Hodder Gibson

Scottish Examination Materials

ADVANCED HIGHER
MATHS
Practice Papers
SECOND EDITION

Peter W. Westwood

Updated by Christine Curran

Orders: please contact Bookpoint Ltd, 130 Milton Park, Abingdon, Oxon OX14 4SB. Telephone: (44) 01235 827720. Fax: (44) 01235 400454. Lines are open 9.00 – 5.00, Monday to Saturday, with a 24-hour message answering service. Visit our website at www.hoddereducation.co.uk. Hodder Gibson can be contacted direct on: Tel: 0141 848 1609; Fax: 0141 889 6315; email: hoddergibson@hodder.co.uk

© Peter W. Westwood, 2003, 2007
First published in 2003 by
Hodder Gibson, an imprint of Hodder Education,
An Hachette Livre UK Company,
2a Christie Street, Paisley PA1 1NB

This edition first published in 2007

Impression number   5 4 3 2 1
Year   2012 2011 2010 2009 2008 2007

Cover photo © Nick Koudis/PhotoDisc
Typeset in 12pt Times by Fakenham Photosetting Limited, Fakenham, Norfolk
Printed and bound in Great Britain by Martins the Printers, Berwick-upon-Twe

A catalogue record for this title is available from the British Library

ISBN-13: 978 0340 968 512

Hodder Gibson
A MEMBER OF THE HODDER HEADLINE GROUP

CONTENTS

PRACTICE UNIT TEST PAPERS

PRACTICE PRELIM PAPERS

PRACTICE FINAL EXAM PAPERS

Advanced Higher
Mathematics

UNIT TEST
(UNIT 1, TEST 1)

NATIONAL
QUALIFICATIONS
Time: 45 minutes

Marks

1. Expand $(p + q)^5$. **(2)**

2. Express $\dfrac{x + 17}{(x - 1)(x + 5)}$ in partial fractions. **(3)**

3. Differentiate with respect to x:

   (a) $3x^4 \ln x$ (b) $\dfrac{3x + 2}{2x + 5}$ (c) $\exp(x + \cos x)$. **(6)**

4. Find   (a) $\displaystyle\int \frac{3x^2}{x^3 - 1}\, dx$ (b) $\displaystyle\int e^{7x}\, dx$. **(4)**

5. Find $\displaystyle\int \sin^4 x \cos x\, dx$ by letting $u = \sin x$. **(3)**

6. Sketch the curve with equation $y = \dfrac{x^2}{x - 1}$ by finding:

   (a) the two asymptotes and how they are approached;

   (b) the intersections with the axes;

   (c) the turning points and justifying their nature. **(9)**

7. Solve, using Gaussian elimination
$$\begin{array}{rcrcrcl} x & & & + & z & = & 1 \\ 3x & + & y & & & = & 1 \\ 2x & + & y & + & z & = & 0 \end{array}$$
(5)

[END OF QUESTION PAPER]

Advanced Higher
Mathematics

UNIT TEST
(UNIT 1, TEST 2)

N A T I O N A L
Q U A L I F I C A T I O N S
Time: 45 minutes

Marks

1. Expand $(2 + y)^4$. **(2)**

2. Express $\dfrac{x + 3}{(x + 1)(x + 2)}$ in partial fractions. **(3)**

3. Differentiate with respect to x:

    (a) $e^x \cos x$ (b) $\dfrac{4x + 5}{7x - 1}$ (c) $\ln(x - \sin x)$. **(6)**

4. Integrate with respect to x (a) $\dfrac{3x^2 + 10x}{x^3 + 5x^2 - 13}$ (b) e^{2x+3}. **(4)**

5. Find $\int \tan^3 x \sec^2 x \, dx$ by letting $u = \tan x$. **(3)**

6. Sketch the curve with equation $y = \dfrac{x^2 - 3x + 6}{x - 2}$ by finding:

    (a) the two asymptotes and how they are approached;

    (b) the intersections with the axes;

    (c) the turning points and justifying their nature. **(9)**

7. Solve, using Gaussian elimination
    $$\begin{aligned} x &+ y &+ 2z &= 15 \\ 6x &- 4y &+ z &= 62 \\ 5x &+ y &- 2z &= 3 \end{aligned}$$. **(5)**

[END OF QUESTION PAPER]

Advanced Higher
Mathematics

UNIT TEST
(UNIT 2, TEST 1)

NATIONAL
QUALIFICATIONS
Time: 45 minutes

Marks

1. Find $\dfrac{d}{dx}(\cos^{-1} x^4)$. **(2)**

2. Using implicit differentiation, find $\dfrac{dy}{dx}$ where $3x^2 - 2y^2 = 11$. **(3)**

3. A curve is defined parametrically by $x = 2t^3$, $y = 2 + t^2$. Find $\dfrac{dy}{dx}$. **(2)**

4. Find $\displaystyle\int \dfrac{4x + 12}{x(x + 4)}\, dx$. **(3)**

5. Use integration by parts to evaluate $\displaystyle\int_0^{\frac{\pi}{2}} x \sin x\, dx$. **(4)**

6. Find the general solution of $\dfrac{dy}{dx} = \dfrac{y}{x^2}$, $x \neq 0$. **(2)**

7. $p = 3 + 2i$, $q = 1 - i$ and $s = 1 - \sqrt{3}\, i$ are complex numbers.

   (*a*) Express pq in the form $x + iy$ and indicate pq on an Argand diagram. **(2)**

   (*b*) Express s in polar form. **(3)**

8. For the arithmetic progression 7, 13, 19, 25, ... find:

   (*a*) the 25th term; **(2)**

   (*b*) the sum of the first 25 terms. **(2)**

Marks

9. For the geometric progression 81, 27, 9, 3, ... find:

    (*a*)   the tenth term; **(2)**

    (*b*)   an expression for the sum of the first *n* terms. **(2)**

10. Disprove the conjecture *bc* is divisible by $a \Rightarrow$ either *b* is divisible by *a* or *c* is divisible by *a*. **(2)**

11. Prove by contradiction that n^2 is odd $\Rightarrow n$ is odd. **(3)**

[END OF QUESTION PAPER]

Advanced Higher
Mathematics

UNIT TEST
(UNIT 2, TEST 2)

NATIONAL
QUALIFICATIONS
Time: 45 minutes

Marks

1. Find $\dfrac{d}{dx}(\tan^{-1} x^2)$. **(2)**

2. For the parabola with equation $y^2 = 16x - 5$, use implicit
    differentiation to find $\dfrac{dy}{dx}$. **(3)**

3. A curve is defined parametrically by $x = t^4, y = 2 + t^3$. Find $\dfrac{dy}{dx}$. **(2)**

4. Find $\displaystyle\int \dfrac{5x - 12}{x(x - 4)}\, dx$. **(3)**

5. Use integration by parts to evaluate $\displaystyle\int_0^1 x\, e^x\, dx$. **(4)**

6. Find the general solution of $\dfrac{dy}{dx} = \dfrac{y}{x^3}, x \neq 0$. **(2)**

7. $u = 2 - 3i, v = 1 + i$ and $w = \sqrt{3} - i$ are complex numbers.

    (a) Express uv in the form $x + iy$ and indicate uv on an Argand dia-
         gram. **(2)**

    (b) Express w in polar form. **(3)**

Marks

8. For the arithmetic progression 4, 9, 14, 19, ... find:

    (*a*)   the 20th term; **(2)**

    (*b*)   the sum of the first 25 terms. **(2)**

9. For the geometric progression 1024, 512, 256, 128, ... find:

    (*a*)   the tenth term; **(2)**

    (*b*)   an expression for the sum of the first *n* terms. **(2)**

10. Find a counter example to show $\sin(x + y) \neq \sin x + \sin y$ for all x, y. **(2)**

11. Prove by contradiction that n^3 is odd $\Rightarrow n$ is odd. **(3)**

[END OF QUESTION PAPER]

Advanced Higher
Mathematics

**UNIT TEST
(UNIT 3, TEST 1)**

NATIONAL
QUALIFICATIONS
Time: 45 minutes

Marks

1. Evaluate $\mathbf{a} \times \mathbf{b}$ where $\mathbf{a} = \begin{pmatrix} 0 \\ 1 \\ 3 \end{pmatrix}$ and $\mathbf{b} = \begin{pmatrix} 2 \\ -1 \\ 1 \end{pmatrix}$.   **(3)**

2. Find the equations of the line passing through C $(2, 1, 3)$ and D $(6, -1, -4)$.   **(2)**

3. Find the equation of the plane which passes through E $(2, -1, 4)$ and has normal vector

$$\mathbf{n} = \begin{pmatrix} 2 \\ 1 \\ -2 \end{pmatrix}.$$ **(2)**

4. $P = \begin{bmatrix} 2 & 1 \\ 3 & 4 \end{bmatrix}$ $Q = \begin{bmatrix} 3 & 2 \\ -6 & 7 \end{bmatrix}$ $R = \begin{bmatrix} 5 & 6 \\ 1 & 2 \end{bmatrix}$ $S = \begin{bmatrix} 2 & 1 & 3 \\ 4 & 1 & 2 \\ 2 & 3 & -1 \end{bmatrix}$

   Evaluate   (a) $3P - 2Q$ (b) PQ (c) R^{-1} (d) $|S|$.   **(1,1,2,2)**

5. Find the first four terms of the Maclaurin expansion for $f(x) = e^{3x}$.   **(4)**

6. The equation $x^3 - 3x + 1 = 0$ can be written as $x = (3x - 1)^{\frac{1}{3}}$.

   By using the simple iterative formula $x_{n+1} = (3x_n - 1)^{\frac{1}{3}}$ with $x_0 = 2$,

   find, correct to two decimal places, the root between 1 and 3.   **(3)**

Marks

7. Solve $\dfrac{dy}{dx} + \dfrac{1}{x}y = \sin x$, $x \neq 0$ giving your answer in the form $y = f(x)$. **(5)**

8. Prove by induction that $\displaystyle\sum_{t=1}^{n} t = \dfrac{1}{2}n(n+1)$. **(5)**

9. Use the Euclidean algorithm to obtain (1961, 518). **(3)**

[END OF QUESTION PAPER]

Advanced Higher
Mathematics

**UNIT TEST
(UNIT 3, TEST 2)**

NATIONAL
QUALIFICATIONS
Time: 45 minutes

Marks

1. Evaluate $\mathbf{a} \times \mathbf{b}$ where $\mathbf{a} = \begin{pmatrix} 3 \\ -2 \\ 1 \end{pmatrix}$ and $\mathbf{b} = \begin{pmatrix} 2 \\ 5 \\ -1 \end{pmatrix}$. **(3)**

2. Find the equations of the line passing through C $(5, -3, 4)$ and D $(7, 2, -1)$. **(2)**

3. Find the equation of the plane which passes through E $(6, -7, 4)$ and has normal vector

   $$\mathbf{n} = \begin{pmatrix} 3 \\ 2 \\ -1 \end{pmatrix}.$$ **(2)**

4. $P = \begin{bmatrix} 3 & 2 \\ 1 & 3 \end{bmatrix}$ $Q = \begin{bmatrix} 4 & -2 \\ 1 & 5 \end{bmatrix}$ $R = \begin{bmatrix} 3 & 5 \\ 5 & 9 \end{bmatrix}$ $S = \begin{bmatrix} 2 & 1 & 3 \\ 4 & -2 & 5 \\ 6 & 0 & 7 \end{bmatrix}$

   Evaluate   (a) $4P - 3Q$ (b) PQ (c) R^{-1} (d) $|S|$. **(1,1,2,2)**

5. Find the first four terms of the Maclaurin expansion for $f(x) = e^{5x}$. **(4)**

6. The equation $x^3 - 4x - 5 = 0$ can be written as $x = (4x + 5)^{\frac{1}{3}}$.

   By using the simple iterative formula $x_{n+1} = (4x_n + 5)^{\frac{1}{3}}$ with $x_0 = 2$,

   find, correct to two decimal places, the root between 1 and 3. **(3)**

11

Marks

7. Solve $\dfrac{dy}{dx} + \dfrac{1}{x}y = \cos x$, $x \neq 0$ giving your answer in the form $y = f(x)$. **(5)**

8. Prove by induction that $\displaystyle\sum_{k=1}^{n} k = \dfrac{1}{2}n(n + 1)$. **(5)**

9. Use the Euclidean algorithm to obtain $(2415, 667)$. **(3)**

[END OF QUESTION PAPER]

PRACTICE PRELIM
PAPERS
(ON UNITS 1 & 2 ONLY)

The time allowed for each of these papers is three hours, which is the length of your final exam.

If you are practising for a two-hour prelim however, you could omit about 33 marks worth of examples with which you are confident, and concentrate on stretching yourself with the others.

On the other hand, you may prefer to work through all the examples but not against the clock.

Instructions to candidates
- Attempt all of the questions.
- Calculators are allowed.
- Full credit is given only where your solution contains appropriate working.
- There is no formulae sheet.

(Note that the instructions on the front of your final exam paper may vary from year to year, so read them carefully.)

Marks

1. Differentiate the following with respect to x:

    (a) $\cos x \sin^{-1} x$ (b) $\dfrac{3x + 2}{x^2 + 1}$ (c) $e^{\sin^2 x}$. **(2, 3, 2)**

2. Integrate by inspection

    (a) $\displaystyle\int 12xe^{\,6x^2+3}\, dx$ (b) $\displaystyle\int \dfrac{3x^2 + 10x}{x^3 + 5x^2 + 11}\, dx$. **(1,1)**

3. Find the geometrical equivalent of each of the following transformations of the Argand plane:-

    (a) $z \rightarrow z + 1 - i$ (b) $z \rightarrow 2iz$ (c) $z \rightarrow 4 - z$. **(1,1,1)**

4. Find the term independent of x in the expansion of $\left(3x^2 + \dfrac{2}{x} \right)^9$. **(4)**

5. Plot the complex numbers $z_1 = 2\,(\cos 30° + i\,\sin 30°)$ and $z_2 = 3\,(\cos 60° + i\,\sin 60°)$ on an Argand diagram and plot the complex number $w = z_1 z_2$ on the same diagram. **(2)**

6. Find the equation of the tangent to the curve with equation $y = x \ln x$ at the point where $x = e$. **(4)**

7. Find the solution of the differential equation $\dfrac{dy}{dx} = \dfrac{x^2}{y} \neq 0$ for which $y = 2$ when $x = 0$. **(3)**

Marks

8. Prove by induction that $\displaystyle\sum_{r=1}^{n} (2r - 1) = n^2$. **(3)**

9. The area enclosed by the x-axis and the lines with equations $x = 3$ and $y = \dfrac{1}{2}x$ is rotated through 2π about the x-axis. Calculate the volume of the solid of revolution so formed. **(4)**

10. (*a*) Obtain partial fractions for $\dfrac{2x + 1}{x^2 + x - 6}$. **(2)**

(*b*) Hence find $\displaystyle\int \dfrac{x^3 + x^2 - 4x + 1}{x^2 + x - 6}\, dx$. **(5)**

11. Find the sum of all the multiples of 7 between 300 and 800. **(5)**

12. Solve $\quad 4x^3 - 12x^2 + 15x - 7 = 0$. **(4)**

13. Integrate with respect to x

$\dfrac{2x + 3}{x^2 + 4x + 8}$ $\quad$ (by re-arranging the numerator and splitting into two integrals). **(5)**

14. Integrate with respect to x

(*a*) $x^2 \sqrt{x^3 + 3}$ $\quad$ (by means of the substitution $u^2 = x^3 + 3$); **(4)**

(*b*) $x^2 \ln x$ $\quad$ (by using integration by parts). **(3)**

Marks

15. (*a*) Express $\dfrac{4(r+1)}{r^2(r+2)^2}$ in partial fractions. **(4)**

(*b*) Hence evaluate $\displaystyle\sum_{r=1}^{n} \dfrac{4(r+1)}{r^2(r+2)^2}$. **(4)**

(*c*) Determine the value of $\displaystyle\sum_{r=1}^{\infty} \dfrac{4(r+1)}{r^2(r+2)^2}$. **(2)**

16. (*a*) Find the modulus and argument of the complex number $z = 4 + 4\sqrt{3}i$ **(3)**

(*b*) Find the three cube roots of z, illustrating them on an Argand diagram. **(7)**

17. One corner, A, of a field consists of two straight hedges, AB and AC, at an angle of 60° to each other.

The fence BC, of length 30 metres, is to be erected to create a triangular enclosure ABC, as shown.

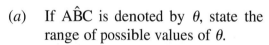
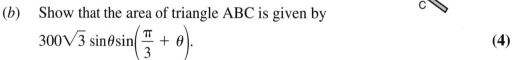

(*a*) If $A\hat{B}C$ is denoted by θ, state the range of possible values of θ. **(1)**

(*b*) Show that the area of triangle ABC is given by
$$300\sqrt{3}\,\sin\theta\sin\!\left(\dfrac{\pi}{3} + \theta\right).$$ **(4)**

(*c*) Find the first and second derivatives of this area function and hence determine the value of θ which corresponds to the greatest area of the enclosure. **(4)**

16

18. A curve is defined parametrically by $x = 3 + \dfrac{4}{t}, y = 4 + \dfrac{3}{t^2}$.

(*a*)   Find the coordinates of the points where the line with equation $y = x$ cuts this curve.   **(3)**

(*b*)   Find the point of intersection of the tangents at these points.   **(5)**

(*c*)   Find an expression for $\dfrac{d^2y}{dx^2}$ and hence make deductions about the shape of the curve.   **(3)**

Total: 100 marks

[END OF QUESTION PAPER]

Advanced Higher Mathematics

PRACTICE PRELIM PAPER NO.2

NATIONAL QUALIFICATIONS
Time: 3 hours

Marks

1. Solve, using Gaussian elimination

$$x + y - z = 3$$
$$2x - 3y + 9z = 60$$
$$7x + 3y + 3z = 69.$$

(5)

2. Differentiate with respect to x:

(a) $\ln(\tan x)$ (b) $e^x \sin x$ (c) $\ln\left(\dfrac{1+x}{1-x}\right)$.

(2,2,4)

3. Evaluate:

(a) $\displaystyle\int_2^4 \frac{x^2 + 3}{x}\, dx$ (b) $\displaystyle\int_{\frac{\pi}{6}}^{\frac{\pi}{3}} \tan^2 x\, dx.$

(4,4)

4. Describe the geometrical equivalent of each of these transformations of the Argand plane:

(a) $f(z) = i\bar{z}$;

(b) $g(z) = wz$ where $w = 3\,(\cos 30° + i \sin 30°)$.

(5)

5. Find the coefficient of x^{10} in the expansion of $\left(3x^2 + \dfrac{4}{x^3}\right)^{10}$.

(4)

6. Express $z = \dfrac{2 + 4i}{1 - 3i}$ in the form $x + iy$ and indicate z *and* $\bar{z}$ on an

   Argand diagram.

(4)

Marks

7. Prove by induction that $\displaystyle\sum_{r=1}^{n} r(3r - 1) = n^2(n + 1)$. **(4)**

8. Verify that the point P $(0, 4)$ lies on each of the curves with equations

    $$y = \frac{19x + 8}{2x^2 + 5x + 2} \quad \text{and} \quad y = \frac{4(4x^2 + 3x - 4)}{5x - 4}$$

    and show that the tangents to these curves at P are at right angles. **(7)**

9. Find the sum of all the multiples of 11 between 500 and 1000. **(5)**

10. Find a general solution of the differential equation

    $\dfrac{dy}{dx} = (x + 2)(y + 1)$ and hence the particular solution for which

    $y = 3$ when $x = 0$. **(4)**

11. (a) Verify that $z = 3$ is a solution of the equation
        $z^3 + z^2 - 7z - 15 = 0$. **(1)**

    (b) Find also the two complex solutions of this equation. **(3)**

12. Find the equation of the tangent to the curve with equation
    $y = (x + 1)^{(x + 2)}$ at the point where the curve crosses the y-axis. **(4)**

13. (a) Use the substitution $u = 2 \cos x$ to evaluate the definite

        integral $\displaystyle\int_{\frac{\pi}{3}}^{\frac{\pi}{2}} \frac{\sin x \, dx}{\sqrt{1 - 4\cos^2 x}}$. **(4)**

    (b) Use integration by parts to find $\displaystyle\int x^3 \ln x \, dx$. **(5)**

19

Marks

14. (*a*) Find a real root of the cubic polynomial
$f(x) = x^3 + 2x^2 - 3x - 10$, and hence factorise $f(x)$ as the product
of a linear factor $p(x)$ and a quadratic factor $q(x)$. **(2)**

(*b*) Prove that $f(x)$ cannot be written as the product of three real linear
factors. **(1)**

(*c*) Use your answer to part (*b*) to express

$$\frac{13x + 8}{x^3 + 2x^2 - 3x - 10} \text{ in the form } \frac{A}{p(x)} + \frac{Bx + C}{q(x)}.$$ **(3)**

(*d*) Hence evaluate $\displaystyle\int \frac{13x + 8}{x^3 + 2x^2 - 3x - 10} \, dx$. **(4)**

15. For the curve with equation $y = \dfrac{(x - 1)^2}{x - 2}$, find $\dfrac{dy}{dx}$ and $\dfrac{d^2y}{dx^2}$ and hence

find the stationary points on the curve and determine their nature. **(10)**

16. (*a*) Write down expressions for   (i) $\displaystyle\sum_{r=1}^{n} r$ (ii) $\displaystyle\sum_{r=1}^{n} r^2$. **(3)**

(*b*) Hence evaluate   (i) $\displaystyle\sum_{r=1}^{n} r(r + 1)$ (ii) $\displaystyle\sum_{r=n+1}^{2n} r^2$. **(6)**

Total: 100 marks

[END OF QUESTION PAPER]

PRACTICE EXAMINATION
PAPERS

The time allowed for each of these papers is three hours, which is the length of your final exam. Every effort has been made to make each reflect the current examination, and so provide you with as much material as possible at the appropriate level of difficulty. Successful performance in Mathematics examinations depends on adequate and appropriate practice. This text supplies these. You have to provide the self-motivation.

Instructions to candidates
- Attempt all the questions.
- Calculators are allowed.
- Full credit is given only where your solution contains appropriate working.
- There is no formulae sheet.

(Note that the instructions on the front of the actual exam paper may vary from year to year, so read them carefully.)

Advanced Higher
Mathematics

**PRACTICE EXAM
PAPER NO. 1**

NATIONAL
QUALIFICATIONS
Time: 3 hours

Marks

1. Use Gaussian elimination to solve the following system of equations:

    $x + 2y - 3z = 10$

    $2x - 3y + 4z = -4$

    $5x - 4y + z = 6.$ **(5)**

2. Expand and simplify $\left(x^3 - \dfrac{3}{x}\right)^5$. **(4)**

3. Express $\dfrac{(x + 2)^2}{x^2(x - 2)}$ in partial fractions. **(4)**

4. A curve has equation $2xy + y^3 = 5$.

    (*a*) Use implicit differentiation to find $\dfrac{dy}{dx}$ (in terms of x and y). **(3)**

    (*b*) Hence find the equation of the tangent to this curve at the point (2, 1). **(2)**

5. The matrix $A = \begin{bmatrix} 2 & -3 \\ 4 & 5 \end{bmatrix}$.

    (*a*) Show that $A^2 = 7A - 22I$.

    (*b*) Hence show that:

    (i) $A^3 = 27A - 154I$ (without evaluating A^3);

    (ii) $A^{-1} = \dfrac{1}{22} (7I - A)$ (without evaluating A^{-1}). **(6)**

Marks

6. Use integration by parts to find $x\sqrt{1 - x}$. **(3)**

7. Evaluate $\displaystyle\int_{\pi}^{\frac{\pi}{-}} \frac{\cos x \, dx}{1 + \sin x}$ by means of the substitution $u = 1 + \sin x$. **(6)**

8. Prove by induction that $5^n + 4n + 7$ is divisible by 4 for all positive integers n. **(5)**

9. Find the stationary value of the function $\dfrac{x - 1}{e^x}$ and determine its nature. **(7)**
   Find also the coordinates of the point of inflexion on the graph of this function.

10. Solve the equation $z^3 = 8$, illustrating the roots on an Argand diagram. **(5)**

11. Find the Maclaurin expansion of $\sec x$ as far as the term in x^4. **(5)**

12. Find the general solution of the differential equation

$$\frac{dy}{dx} = \frac{y - y^2}{x^2} \, , \ x \neq 0 \text{ expressing } y \text{ as a function of } x.$$ **(5)**

13. Let $u_1, u_2, u_3, \ldots$ be an arithmetic sequence and $v_1, v_2, v_3, \ldots$ be a geometric sequence.

   (*a*) If $u_3 = 11$ and $u_7 = 23$, find the values of u_6 and u_{10}. **(2)**

   (*b*) If $v_1 = u_{10}$ and $v_2 = u_6$, find the sum to infinity of the geometric sequence. **(5)**

   (*c*) Hence find a formula for Vn in terms of n. **(2)**

23

Marks

14. A curve is defined parametrically by the equations

$x = 8 - \dfrac{1}{t^3}$, $y = t^3 - 1$ (t ≠ 0).

(*a*) Show that this curve cuts the *x*-axis only once and the *y*-axis only once, stating the coordinates of these points. **(2)**

(*b*) Find the equations of the tangents at these points and show that they intersect on the line with equation $x + 8y = 0$. **(7)**

(*c*) Show also that there are no points of inflexion on this curve. **(3)**

15. (*a*) Find the general solution of $\dfrac{dy}{dx} + \dfrac{y}{x} = x^2$. **(4)**

(*b*) Find the particular integral for which $x = 4$ and $y = 20$. **(2)**

(*c*) Find the solution of the differential equation

$\dfrac{d^2y}{dx^2} - 4\dfrac{dy}{dx} + 13y = 0$. **(4)**

16. The plane π_1 contains the points A (1, 2, 10), B (−2, 4, −6) and C (0, 3, 5).

The plane π_2 has equation $2x - y + 3z = 16$.

(*a*) Find the equation of the plane π_1. **(3)**

(*b*) Find the equations of the line of intersection of the planes π_1 and π_2. **(4)**

(*c*) Find the equations of the line passing through B and perpendicular to the plane π_2, where this line meets the plane. **(2)**

Total: 100 marks

[END OF QUESTION PAPER]

Advanced Higher Mathematics

PRACTICE EXAM PAPER NO. 2

NATIONAL QUALIFICATIONS

Time: 3 hours

Marks

1. Use Gaussian elimination to solve the following system of equations

$$x - y + 2z = 5$$
$$2x + y - z = 3$$
$$3x + 2y - 2z = 3.$$

   (5)

2. For any angle x, the matrices $A(x)$ and $B(x)$ are defined by

$$A(x) = \begin{bmatrix} \cos x & -\sin x \\ \sin x & \cos x \end{bmatrix} \quad \text{and} \quad B(x) = \begin{bmatrix} \sin x & \cos x \\ \cos x & -\sin x \end{bmatrix}.$$

   Prove that: (a) $[A(x)]^2 = A(2x)$;   **(2)**

   (b) $[B(x)]^2 = I$ where I is the 2×2 unit matrix.   **(2)**

3. Describe these transformations of the Argand plane in geometrical terms:

   (a) $f(z) = \bar{z}$ (b) $g(z) = iz$ (c) $h(z) = 2 - z$.   **(4)**

4. Find term in x^4 in the expansion of $\left(x - \dfrac{1}{x}\right)^{10}$.   **(4)**

5. Prove that the derivative with respect to x of $\tan^{-1}\left(\dfrac{1 + x}{1 - x}\right)$ is the same as the derivative of $\tan^{-1} x$.   **(5)**

Marks

6. Find $\int \dfrac{dx}{x^{\frac{1}{2}} - x^{\frac{1}{4}}}$ by using the substitution $x = z^4$. (5)

7. Show that if $(x + y)^4 = 4xy$, then $\dfrac{dy}{dx} = \dfrac{y(3x - y)}{x(x - 3y)}$. (5)

8. Prove by induction that $4^n + 6n + 8$ is divisible by 9 for all positive integers n. (7)

9. Find the stationary points on the curve with equation $y = x^3(x + 4)$ and determine their nature. (5)

10. By writing $(k + 1)^2 - k^2 = 2k + 1$, show that

$$\sum_{k=1}^{n} \{(k + 1)^2 - k^2\} = n + 2\sum_{k=1}^{n} k.$$

Hence show that $\displaystyle\sum_{k=1}^{n} k = \dfrac{n(n + 1)}{2}$. (5)

11. Obtain the Maclaurin expansion of $\ln(1 + \sin x)$ as far as the term in x^4. (5)

12. (*a*) Prove directly that 6 is a factor of $n^3 - n$ for all integers n. (2)

    (*b*) Decide whether each of the following is true or false, giving a proof or counter example as appropriate:

        (i)   if a, b are integers such that ab is odd, then a and b are both odd (2)

        (ii)   if p, q, r are integers such that p is a factor of qr, then p is a factor of either q or r. (2)

13. Newton's law of cooling states that the rate of change of the temperature of a mug of coffee is proportional to the difference in temperature
of the coffee and the ambient air.

Let the coffee be at $T°C$ at time t minutes and the ambient air be at $a°C$.

    (*a*)   Write down an expression for $\dfrac{dT}{dt}$ to model this situation.   **(2)**

    (*b*)   Find the general solution of this differential equation.   **(3)**

    (*c*)   When the room temperature is 60°C, the coffee cools from 90°C
to 80°C in 2 minutes.
How much longer will it take the coffee to cool to 70°C?   **(5)**

14. Find the general solution of the differential equation

$$\frac{d^2y}{dx^2} - 7\frac{dy}{dx} + 10y = 10x^2 - 14x + 22.$$ **(7)**

Determine the solution for which $y(0) = 1 = y'(0)$.   **(3)**

15. (*a*)   Find the coordinates of the point A in which the line l with

equations $\dfrac{x-1}{2} = \dfrac{y}{-3} = \dfrac{z+2}{-1}$ meets the plane π_1 with

equation $x + 2y + z = 4$.   **(3)**

    (*b*)   Show that the equation of the plane π_2 which contains l and is
perpendicular to π_1 is $x + 3y - 7z = 15$.   **(3)**

    (*c*)   Find the equations of the line of intersection of the planes π_1 and
π_2.   **(4)**

Marks

16. Obtain partial fractions for $\dfrac{x(x - 3)}{(x + 3)(x^2 + 9)}$ **(4)**

and hence show that $\displaystyle\int_3^9 \dfrac{x(x - 3)}{(x + 3)(x^2 + 9)} \, dx = \ln 2 + \dfrac{\pi}{4} - \tan^{-1} 3.$ **(6)**

Total: 100 marks

[END OF QUESTION PAPER]

Advanced Higher
Mathematics

**PRACTICE EXAM
PAPER NO. 3**

NATIONAL
QUALIFICATIONS
Time: 3 hours

Marks

1. Find the term independent of x in the expansion of $\left(\dfrac{x^2}{2} + \dfrac{3}{x^3}\right)^{10}$. **(4)**

2. Use integration by parts to evaluate $\displaystyle\int_0^{\pi} x\,\sin 2x\,dx$. **(4)**

3. Differentiate $x^3 \sin^2 3x$ with respect to x, and simplify. **(4)**

4. Compare and discuss the exact solutions of these two systems of equations:

    (a) $\begin{cases} x + 2y = 6 \\ x + 1{\cdot}999\,y = 5{\cdot}999 \end{cases}$ (b) $\begin{cases} x + 2y = 6 \\ x + 2{\cdot}0001y = 6{\cdot}0004 \end{cases}$. **(5)**

5. A curve is defined parametrically by $x = a(\sec\theta + \tan\theta)$, $y = b(\sec\theta - \tan\theta)$.

    Show that at the point where $\theta = \dfrac{\pi}{4}$, the gradient of the curve

    is given by $\dfrac{b}{a}\,(2\sqrt{2} - 3)$. **(4)**

6. Given that $\mathbf{a} = 2\mathbf{i} + 3\mathbf{j} - 4\mathbf{k}$, $\mathbf{b} = 2\mathbf{i} - \mathbf{j} + \mathbf{k}$, $\mathbf{c} = 3\mathbf{i} + 2\mathbf{j} - \mathbf{k}$, and $\mathbf{d} = \mathbf{i} - 2\mathbf{j} + t\mathbf{k}$:

    (a) evaluate $\mathbf{a}.(\mathbf{b} \times \mathbf{c})$; **(2)**

    (b) find the value of t for which $\mathbf{a}.(\mathbf{b} \times \mathbf{d}) = 1$. **(2)**

Marks

7. The matrix $A = \begin{bmatrix} 5 & 6 \\ 3 & 4 \end{bmatrix}$. Show that:

    (*a*) $A^2 = 9A - 2I$;   **(2)**

    (*b*) $A^3 = 79A - 18I$ (without evaluating A^3);   **(2)**

    (*c*) $A^{-1} = \dfrac{1}{2}(9I - A)$ (without evaluating A^{-1}).   **(2)**

8. The area bounded by the *x*-axis, the curve with equation $y = \dfrac{1}{3}x^2 + 1$, and the ordinates $x = 1$ and $x = 3$ is rotated through 2π about the *x*-axis. Calculate the volume of the solid of revolution so formed.   **(4)**

9. Prove by induction that $\displaystyle\sum_{r=1}^{n} \frac{1}{(3r - 2)(3r + 1)} = \frac{n}{3n + 1}$.   **(5)**

10. An ancient druid tribe built 100 seats in a circle round their new altar for their first May Day celebrations. For the following May Day, they built another ring of 110 seats round the first ring. They built a further ring of 120 seats round that for the following year, and so on.

    (*a*)   Find the total number of seats round the altar for the nth May Day at the new altar.   **(3)**

    (*b*)   How many years would have to pass before the number of seats exceeded 2000?   **(2)**

11. Express $\dfrac{3x + 4}{x^2(x^2 + 1)}$ in partial fractions.   **(6)**

12. (*a*) Show that the equation $2x^3 - 4x^2 + 3x - 5 = 0$ has a root between 1 and 2, and determine its value correct to one decimal place. **(2)**

(*b*) Establish the iteration formula $x_{n+1} = \dfrac{4x_n{}^2 - 3x_n + 5}{2x_n{}^2}$

and use it to find this root correct to 3 decimal places. **(3)**

13. Use the Euclidean algorithm to find integers x and y such that $34x + 111y = 1$. **(4)**

14. A curve has equation $y = \dfrac{4x^2 - 3}{x^3}$.

(*a*) Find equations of both asymptotes. **(4)**

(*b*) Find the stationary points and determine their nature. **(4)**

(*c*) Sketch the curve. **(2)**

15. Let $z = \cos\theta + i\sin\theta$.

(*a*) Use the binomial theorem to show that the real part of z^5 is

$\cos^5\theta - 10\cos^3\theta\sin^2\theta + 5\cos\theta\sin^4\theta$. **(4)**

(*b*) Use de Moivre's theorem to write down an expression for z^5 in terms of 5θ. **(1)**

(*c*) Use your answers to parts (*a*) and (*b*) to express:

(i) $\cos 5\theta$ in terms of $\cos\theta$;

(ii) $\sin 5\theta$ in terms of $\sin\theta$. **(2)**

(*d*) Hence show that $\tan 5\theta = \dfrac{\tan^5\theta - 10\tan^3\theta + 5\tan\theta}{1 - 10\tan^2\theta + 5\tan^4\theta}$. **(3)**

Marks

16. (*a*) Find the solution of the differential equation

$$\frac{d^2y}{dx^2} + \frac{dy}{dx} - 12y = 0 \text{ for which } y(0) = 7 = y'(0).$$ **(5)**

(*b*) Find the general solution of the differential equation

$$\frac{dy}{dx} + \frac{3y}{x+2} = x + 2, x \neq -2$$

and the particular solution for which $x = -1$ when $y = 1$. **(6)**

17. (*a*) Find an equation of the plane containing the points A (1, 0, 1), B (0, 2, 1) and C (-1, 0, 2). **(4)**

(*b*) Find an equation of the line of intersection of the plane with equation $2x + y + 4z = 6$ and the plane with normal vector $\mathbf{i} + \mathbf{j} - 2\mathbf{k}$ through the point (1, 1, 1). **(5)**

Total: 100 marks

[END OF QUESTION PAPER]

Marks

1. Use Gaussian elimination to show that the following system of equations does not have a unique solution, and describe the solution set

$$
\begin{aligned}
x &+ 2y - 3z = 15 \\
2x &- y + 2z = -1 \\
5x &+ z = 13 .
\end{aligned}
$$

    (6)

2. Express $\dfrac{2x^2 - 1}{x^2 (x - 1)}$ in partial fractions. **(5)**

3. (*a*) Integrate $\dfrac{x^2 + 3x + 6}{x^2 + 4}$ with respect to x. **(4)**

    (*b*) Differentiate $x^2 \sin^{-1} x$ with respect to x. **(3)**

4. Find the equation of the tangent to the curve with equation

    $x^3 + 2x^2 y^2 = 16$ at the point $(2, 1)$. **(6)**

5. Find the solution of the differential equation

    $\dfrac{dy}{dx} = \sin x \sec y$

    for which $y = \dfrac{\pi}{6}$ when $x = \dfrac{\pi}{3}$. **(5)**

6. (a) Obtain an expression for $z^4 + z^3 + z^2 + z + 1$ as five terms of a geometric series.

(b) Hence solve the equation $z^4 + z^3 + z^2 + z + 1 = 0$.

(c) Hence find real quadratic factors for $z^4 + z^3 + z^2 + z + 1$. **(7)**

7. Let $A = \begin{bmatrix} 2 & -2 & 0 \\ 1 & 0 & 2 \\ -2 & 2 & 0 \end{bmatrix}$.

Write down the matrix $A - \lambda I$ where $\lambda \in \mathbb{R}$ and I is the 3×3 identity matrix.

Find the values of λ for which the determinant of $A - \lambda I$ is zero. **(5)**

8. Prove by induction that $5^n + 12n - 1$ is divisible by 16 for all positive integral values of n. **(7)**

9. State the converse of the proposition: $a < a^3 \Rightarrow a < a^2$, and decide whether the converse is true or false, proving or disproving it by providing a counter example. **(3)**

10. Obtain the Maclaurin expansion of $\ln(\cos^2 x)$ as far as the term in x^4. **(5)**

11. Use the Euclidean algorithm to find integers x and y such that $172x + 159y = 1$. **(4)**

Marks

12. For the curve with equation $y = \dfrac{4x}{(2 - x)^2}$ determine:

    (a) the equation of any asymptotes; **(4)**

    (b) the coordinates of the turning point and its nature; **(4)**

    (c) the appearance of the curve by a sketch. **(2)**

13. (a) Express $\dfrac{1}{r^2 + 5r + 6}$ in partial fractions. **(4)**

    (b) Hence evaluate $\displaystyle\sum_{r=1}^{n} \dfrac{1}{r^2 + 5r + 6}$, expressing your answer as a single fraction. **(4)**

    (c) Hence evaluate $\displaystyle\sum_{r=n+1}^{2n} \dfrac{1}{r^2 + 5r + 6}$. **(2)**

14. (a) Show that the lines $l_1: \dfrac{x - 2}{2} = \dfrac{y + 1}{1} = \dfrac{z - 3}{-1}$

    and $l_2: \dfrac{x - 5}{1} = \dfrac{y + 3}{-3} = \dfrac{z - 4}{2}$

    intersect, and find their point of intersection. **(4)**

    (b) Find the equation of the plane which contains l_1 and l_2. **(3)**

    (c) Find the size of the acute angle between l_1 and l_2. **(3)**

Marks

15. (*a*) Find the general solution of the differential equation

$$\frac{d^2y}{dx^2} - 6\frac{dy}{dx} + 9y = e^{2x}.$$ **(7)**

(*b*) Find the solution for which $y(0) = 2$ and $y'(0) = 7$. **(3)**

Total: 100 marks

[END OF QUESTION PAPER]

Advanced Higher Mathematics   **PRACTICE EXAM PAPER NO. 5**   NATIONAL QUALIFICATIONS

Time: 3 hours

Marks

1. Express $\dfrac{4x^2 - 4}{x^2(x - 2)}$ in partial fractions. **(5)**

2. Two matrices are defined as $A = \begin{pmatrix} 1 & -1 & 1 \\ 2 & 1 & 3 \\ -1 & 1 & 1 \end{pmatrix}$

   and $B = \begin{pmatrix} -2 & 2 & -4 \\ -5 & 2 & -1 \\ 3 & 0 & 3 \end{pmatrix}$.

   (a) Show that $AB = kI$ where k is a constant. **(2)**

   (b) Hence find A^{-1}. **(1)**

3. Evaluate $\displaystyle\int_0^{\frac{\pi}{5}} 3x \cos 5x\, dx$. **(4)**

4. Solve $\begin{cases} 3x + 4y = 17 \\ 2{\cdot}999x + 4y = 17{\cdot}001 \end{cases}$

   Discuss the effect of replacing the $17{\cdot}001$ by $16{\cdot}993$. **(4)**

5. Find the coefficient of x^9 in the expansion of $\left(2x^2 + \dfrac{3}{x}\right)^9$. **(5)**

6. A particle moving in a plane is governed by the laws
$$x = t + \sin t \qquad y = t - \cos t.$$

    (*a*)   Show that the speed can be expressed as $\sqrt{3 + 2(x - y)}$. **(3)**

    (*b*)   Show that the magnitude of the acceleration is constant. **(2)**

7. Oil is dripping on to a garage floor and making an ever-increasing circular stain.

    When the radius of the stain is 3 cm, the radius is increasing at the rate of 0·2 cm/s.

    Calculate the rate at which the area is increasing at that time. **(4)**

8. Prove by induction $\displaystyle\sum_{r=1}^{n}(-1)^{r-1}\,\frac{2r+1}{r(r+1)} = \frac{(-1)^{n-1}}{n+1} + 1$. **(4)**

9. Find the third term of the geometric sequence whose second term is 300 and whose sum to infinity is 1600. [There are two possible answers.] **(7)**

10. Find the solution of the differential equation $\dfrac{d^2y}{dx^2} - 10\dfrac{dy}{dx} + 25y = 0$, for which $y = 0$ and $y' = 2$ when $x = 0$. **(4)**

11. Find the Maclaurin expansion of $(2 + x)^2\,e^{-x}$ as far as the term in x^3. **(5)**

12. (*a*)   Prove that if a and b are odd integers, then $(a^2 + b^2)$ is divisible by 2 but not by 4. **(3)**

    (*b*)   State the converse of this result, and say whether it is true or false. Give a proof or counter-example as appropriate. **(3)**

Marks

13. Find the general solution of the differential equation

$$\frac{dy}{dx} - y \cot x = x \sin^2 x.$$ **(4)**

14. A channel to carry rainwater is to be constructed along the foot of a motorway banking. It is to consist of sets of four concrete slabs each 0.5 m wide. Two are laid horizontally, and two laid at an angle θ to the vertical, as shown, to form a cross-section in the shape of an isosceles trapezium.

(*a*) Express the cross-sectional area of the channel in terms of θ, where $0 \leqslant \theta \leqslant \frac{\pi}{2}$. **(3)**

(*b*) Show that the value of θ for which the channel can carry the greatest volume of rainwater is given by $\theta = \sin^{-1}\left(\frac{\sqrt{3} - 1}{2}\right)$, justifying the nature of your answer. **(6)**

(*c*) Show that the corresponding cross-sectional area is given by $\frac{(3 + \sqrt{3})\sqrt{\sqrt{3}}}{8\sqrt{2}}$ m². **(1)**

Marks

15. An infection hits an ant colony. Let p denote the percentage of ants infected after t days.

The spread of the infection can be modelled by $\dfrac{dp}{dt} = kp(100 - p)$, where k is a constant.

   (*a*) Show that the general solution of this differential equation can be written as

$$p = \frac{100}{1 + Ae^{-100kt}} \text{ where } A \text{ is a constant.}$$

(**6**)

   (*b*) Given that 10% of the ants are infected after 2 days, and 15% after 3 days, find the value of k.

(**4**)

16. Show that $(1 + i)$ is a root of $z^4 + 4 = 0$ and hence find all the roots, illustrating them on an Argand diagram.

On the same diagram, label the points which represent the squares of these roots.

(**10**)

17. A is the point $(12, 5, -2)$, B $(20, 6, -6)$, C $(-1, -6, -3)$ and D $(7, 10, 5)$.

   (*a*) Find the equations of the lines AB and CD.

(**4**)

   (*b*) Show that AB and CD intersect, giving the coordinates of the point of intersection.

(**3**)

   (*c*) Find the equation of the plane containing AB and CD.

(**3**)

Total: 100 marks

[END OF QUESTION PAPER]

Advanced Higher
Mathematics

PRACTICE EXAM
PAPER NO. 6

NATIONAL
QUALIFICATIONS
Time: 3 hours

Marks

1. How many solutions does the given system of equations have?

$$2x + 3y + 4z = 1$$
$$5x + 6y + 7z = 2$$
$$8x + 9y + 10z = 4$$

(4)

2. The matrices A and B are given by $A = \begin{bmatrix} 2 & 3 & -1 \\ 1 & -1 & 0 \\ 1 & -2 & 3 \end{bmatrix}$

and $B = \begin{bmatrix} -2 & 1 & 3 \\ 1 & 0 & 1 \\ 2 & -3 & 1 \end{bmatrix}$.

If $C = AB$, evaluate the determinant of C.

(5)

3. Differentiate $\tan^{-1}\left(\dfrac{1 + \sin x}{1 - \cos x}\right)$ with respect to x, and simplify.

(5)

4. Use the substitution $x = 3\sin t$ to integrate $\dfrac{2x - 1}{\sqrt{9 - x^2}}$ with respect to x.

(4)

5. Find the general solution of the differential equation

$$\frac{d^2y}{dx^2} - 10\frac{dy}{dx} + 29y = 4\cos 5x + 50\sin 5x.$$

(6)

Marks

6. Find the general solution of the differential equation $(1 + x^2) \dfrac{dy}{dx} = 2y$ and find the particular solution for which $y = 3$ when $x = 0$. **(5)**

7. (*a*) Find the 2×2 matrix associated with reflection in the line with equation $y = -x$. **(2)**

   (*b*) Hence find the image of the point $(2, 1)$ under this reflection. **(1)**

8. Use logarithmic differentiation to find $\dfrac{dy}{dx}$ where $y = \dfrac{1 - \cos x}{1 + \sin x}$. **(5)**

9. Prove by induction that $\displaystyle\sum_{r=1}^{n} (6r + 1) = n(3n + 4)$. **(5)**

10. (*a*) For $f(x) = \dfrac{e^x}{x}$, find $\dfrac{df}{dx}$ and $\dfrac{d^2f}{dx^2}$. **(5)**

    (*b*) Determine the nature of the stationary value of f. **(2)**

11. Use the Euclidean algorithm to find integers p and q such that $43p + 11q = 1$. **(4)**

12. Expand using the binomial theorem $\left(3a - \dfrac{4}{b}\right)^3$ **(3)**

13. (*a*) Find the Maclaurin expansion of e^x up to terms in x^3. **(1)**

    (*b*) Hence write down the expansion of e^{x^3}. **(1)**

    (*c*) Using the above answers, find e^{x+x^3} up to terms in x^3. **(2)**

Marks

14. (*a*) Find the fourth roots of $i - \sqrt{3}$. **(6)**

(*b*) Find the modulus and argument of $\dfrac{(2 - i)^2(1 - 3i)}{3 + i}$. **(6)**

15. (*a*) Express $\dfrac{1}{r^2 + 7r + 12}$ in partial fractions. **(4)**

(*b*) Hence evaluate $\displaystyle\sum_{r=1}^{n} \dfrac{1}{r^2 + 7r + 12}$, expressing your answer as a single fraction. **(4)**

(*c*) Hence evaluate $\displaystyle\sum_{r=11}^{20} \dfrac{1}{r^2 + 7r + 12}$ exactly. **(2)**

16. Obtain partial fractions for $\dfrac{x + 2}{x(x^2 + 1)}$ and hence evaluate

$$\int_{1}^{\sqrt{3}} \dfrac{x + 2}{x(x^2 + 1)}\, dx. \qquad \textbf{(9)}$$

17. P is the point $(3, -1, -1)$, Q $(1, -2, 1)$ and R $(4, 0, 5)$.

(*a*) Show that ΔPQR is right-angled. **(3)**

(*b*) Write down the equations of the hypotenuse. **(2)**

(*c*) Does the origin lie on the hypotenuse? **(1)**

(*d*) Find the equation of the plane PQR. **(3)**

Total: 100 marks

[END OF QUESTION PAPER]

UNIT 1, TEST 1
SOLUTIONS

1. Refer to Pascal's triangle for the coefficients

$$(p + q)^5 = 1\, p^5\, q^0 + 5\, p^4\, q + 10\, p^3\, q^2 + 10\, p^2\, q^3 + 5\, p\, q^4 + 1\, p^0\, q^5$$

$$= p^5 + 5p^4q + 10p^3q^2 + 10p^2q^3 + 5pq^4 + q^5.$$

```
              1
            1   1
          1   2   1
        1   3   3   1
      1   4   6   4   1
    1   5  10  10   5   1
```

2. Let $\dfrac{x + 17}{(x - 1)(x + 5)} \equiv \dfrac{A}{(x - 1)} + \dfrac{B}{(x + 5)}$. Now multiply both sides by $(x - 1)(x + 5)$

so $x + 17 \equiv A(x + 5) + B(x - 1)$

$x = 1 \Rightarrow 18 = 6A \Rightarrow A = 3$

$x = -5 \Rightarrow 12 = -6B \Rightarrow B = -2$ $\qquad$ hence $\dfrac{3}{(x - 1)} - \dfrac{2}{(x + 5)}$

Check your answer before moving on by finding first the common denominator.

3. (a) $D(3x^4 \ln x) = 3x^4 \dfrac{1}{x} + 12x^3 \ln x = 3x^3 + 12x^3 \ln x = 3x^3(1 + 4 \ln x).$

(b) $D\left(\dfrac{3x + 2}{2x + 5}\right) = \dfrac{(2x + 5)(3) - (3x + 2)(2)}{(2x + 5)^2} = \dfrac{11}{(2x + 5)^2}.$

(c) $D(e^{(x + \cos x)}) = e^{(x + \cos x)} D(x + \cos x) = (1 - \sin x)e^{(x + \cos x)}.$

4. (a) $\displaystyle\int \dfrac{3x^2 dx}{x^3 - 1} = \ln(x^3 - 1) + c$ (Note: The top line is the derivative of the bottom line. Check by differentiating.)

(b) $\displaystyle\int e^{7x}\, dx = \dfrac{1}{7} e^{7x} + c.$

5. let $u = \sin x$

$\therefore du = \cos x\, dx \Rightarrow \displaystyle\int \sin^4 x \cos x\, dx = \int u^4\, du = \dfrac{1}{5} u^5 + c = \dfrac{1}{5} \sin^5 x + c.$

6. (a) $y = \dfrac{x^2}{x-1} = \dfrac{x^2 - x + x}{x-1} = x + \dfrac{x}{x-1} = x + \dfrac{x-1+1}{x-1} = x + 1 + \dfrac{1}{x-1}$

$x = 1$ is an asymptote $y = x + 1$ is an asymptote

$x = 1 - \epsilon \Rightarrow y = (+ve)/-\epsilon \, (<0)$ $x \to -\infty \Rightarrow y = x + 1 + 1/(-ve) < x + 1$

$x = 1 + \epsilon \Rightarrow y = (+ve)/+\epsilon \, (>0)$ $x \to +\infty \Rightarrow y = x + 1 + 1/(+ve) > x + 1$

(b) $x = 0 \Rightarrow y = 0$ $(y = x + 1)$

$\quad y = 0 \Rightarrow x = 0.$ $(x = 1)$

(c) $\dfrac{dy}{dx} = 1 - (x-1)^{-2} = 1 - \dfrac{1}{(x-1)^2} = 0$ for stationary points

$\Rightarrow (x-1)^2 = 1 \Rightarrow x - 1 = \pm 1 \Rightarrow x = 0, 2 \Rightarrow y = 0, 4 \Rightarrow (0, 0), (2, 4)$ are the stat. points.

$\dfrac{d^2y}{dx^2} = \dfrac{d}{dx}(1 - (x-1)^{-2}) = 2(x-1)^{-3} = \dfrac{2}{(x-1)^3}$

$y''(0) = -2 < 0 \Rightarrow (0, 0)$ is a maximum turning point
$y''(2) = 2 > 0 \Rightarrow (2, 4)$ is a minimum turning point.

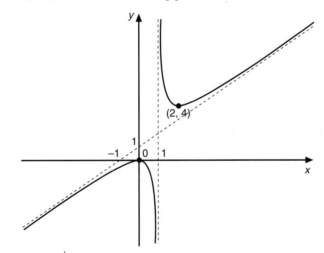

7.

	1	0	1	1
	3	1	0	1
	2	1	1	0
$r_2 - 3\,r_1$	0	1	-3	-2
$r_3 - 2\,r_1$	0	1	-1	-2
$r_5 - r_4$	0	0	2	0

$r_5 - r_4 \quad \Rightarrow 2z = 0 \qquad\qquad \Rightarrow z = 0$

$r_4 \quad \Rightarrow y - 3(0) = -2 \quad \Rightarrow y = -2$

$r_1 \quad \Rightarrow x + 0 + 0 = 1 \quad \Rightarrow x = 1$

$\Rightarrow (x, y, z) = (1, -2, 0)$

UNIT 1 TEST 2
ANSWERS

1. $16 + 32\,y + 24\,y^2 + 8\,y^3 + y^4$.

2. $\dfrac{2}{x+1} - \dfrac{1}{x+2}$.

3. (*a*) $e^x\,(\cos x - \sin x)$ (*b*) $\dfrac{-39}{(7x-1)^2}$ (*c*) $\dfrac{1 - \cos x}{x - \sin x}$.

4. (*a*) $\ln(x^3 + 5x^2 - 13) + c$

    (*b*) $\dfrac{1}{2}\,e^{(2x+3)} + c$.

5. $\dfrac{1}{4}\tan^4 x + c$.

6. (*a*) $x = 2,\ y = x - 1$
    (*b*) $(0, -3)$, none with Ox
    (*c*) $(0, -3)$ max
       $(4, 5)$ min.

7. $(x, y, z) = (5, -6, 8)$.

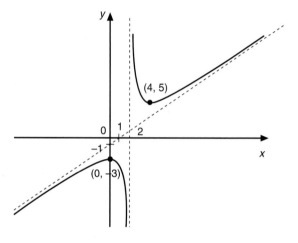

UNIT 2, TEST 1
SOLUTIONS

1. $D(\cos^{-1} x^4) = \dfrac{-1}{\sqrt{1 - (x^4)^2}}\, 4x^3 = \dfrac{-4x^3}{\sqrt{1 - x^8}}$.

2. $3x^2 - 2y^2 = 11 \Rightarrow 6x - 4y\, y' = 0 \Rightarrow y' = \dfrac{6x}{4y} = \dfrac{3x}{2y}$.

3. $x = 2t^3 \quad\Rightarrow\quad \dfrac{dx}{dt} = 6t^2 \qquad y = 2 + t^2 \quad\Rightarrow\quad \dfrac{dy}{dt} = 2t$

$$\Rightarrow \dfrac{dy}{dx} = \dfrac{dy}{dt}\dfrac{dt}{dx} = \dfrac{dy}{dt} \div \dfrac{dx}{dt} = \dfrac{2t}{6t^2} = \dfrac{1}{3t}\, .$$

4. let $\dfrac{4x + 12}{x(x + 4)} \equiv \dfrac{A}{x} + \dfrac{B}{x + 4}$ so $4x + 12 \equiv A(x + 4) + Bx$

$x = 0 \Rightarrow 12 = 4A \Rightarrow A = 3$

$x = -4 \Rightarrow -4 = -4B \Rightarrow B = 1$

$$\Rightarrow \dfrac{4x + 12}{x(x + 4)} = \dfrac{3}{x} + \dfrac{1}{x + 4}$$

$$\Rightarrow \int \dfrac{4x + 12}{x(x + 4)}\, dx = \int \dfrac{3}{x} + \dfrac{1}{x + 4}\, dx = 3\int \dfrac{1}{x}\, dx + \int \dfrac{1}{x + 4}\, dx$$

$$= 3\ln x + \ln (x + 4) + c \quad (= \ln kx^3(x + 4)).$$

5. $\displaystyle\int_0^{\frac{\pi}{2}} x \sin x\, dx = \int_0^{\frac{\pi}{2}} xD(-\cos x)dx = [-x \cos x]_0^{\frac{\pi}{2}} - (-)\int_0^{\frac{\pi}{2}} - \cos x\, D(x)\, dx$

$$= [0 - 0] + [\sin x]_0^{\frac{\pi}{2}} = 1 - 0 = 1.$$

6. $\dfrac{dy}{dx} = \dfrac{y}{x^2} \Rightarrow \dfrac{dy}{y} = \dfrac{dx}{x^2} \Rightarrow \int\dfrac{dy}{y} = \int\dfrac{dx}{x^2} \Rightarrow \ln y = \dfrac{x^{-1}}{-1} + c = c - \dfrac{1}{x}$

$$\Rightarrow y = e^{c - \frac{1}{x}} = e^c\, e^{-\frac{1}{x}} = Ae^{-\frac{1}{x}}\, .$$

7. (a) $pq = (3 + 2i)(1 - i) = 3 - 2(-1) + 2i - 3i = 5 - i$

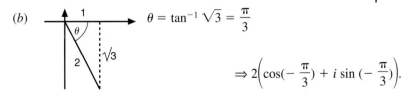

(b) $\theta = \tan^{-1} \sqrt{3} = \dfrac{\pi}{3}$

$$\Rightarrow 2\left(\cos\left(-\dfrac{\pi}{3}\right) + i \sin \left(-\dfrac{\pi}{3}\right)\right).$$

8. (a) 'a' = 7 'd' = 6 $\Rightarrow$ $T_{25} = a + 24d = 7 + 24 \times 6 = 151$.

(b) $S_n = \dfrac{n}{2} [2a + (n-1)d] = \dfrac{25}{2} [2 \times 7 + 24 \times 6] = 25[7 + 72] = 7900 \div 4 = 1975$.

9. (a) 'a' = 81 'r' = $\dfrac{1}{3}$ $\Rightarrow$ $T_{10} = ar^9 = 81(\dfrac{1}{3})^9 = 3^4 \div 3^9 = 3^{-5} = \dfrac{1}{243}$.

(b) $S_n = \dfrac{a(1 - r^n)}{1 - r} = \dfrac{81\left(1 - \left(\dfrac{1}{3}\right)^n\right)}{1 - \dfrac{1}{3}} = \dfrac{243}{2} \left(1 - \dfrac{1}{3^n}\right)$.

10. 6 | 90 $\Rightarrow$ 6 | 9 $\times$ 10, but 6 does not divide 9 or 10.

11. Suppose that n^2 is odd and n is even

then, n is even $\Rightarrow$ $n = 2m$ for some $m \in Z \Rightarrow n^2 = (2m)^2 = 4m^2 = 2(2m^2)$ which is even i.e. n^2 is odd and n^2 is even (which is a contradiction), hence result.

UNIT 2 TEST 2
ANSWERS

1. $\dfrac{2x}{1 + x^4}$.

2. $y' = \dfrac{8}{y}$.

3. $\dfrac{3}{4t}$.

4. $3\ln x + 2\ln(x - 4) + c$.

5. 1.

6. $y = Ae - \dfrac{1}{2x^2}$.

7. (*a*) $5 - i$ (*b*) $2\left[\cos(-\dfrac{\pi}{6}) + i\sin(-\dfrac{\pi}{6})\right]$.
    (Same diagram as in Q7(a) previous test.)

8. (*a*)   99   (*b*)   1600.

9. (*a*)   2   (*b*) $2048\left(1 - \dfrac{1}{2^n}\right)$.

10. e.g. $x = 30°$ and $y = 60°$.

11. suppose n^3 is odd and n is even, ...

UNIT 3 TEST 1
SOLUTIONS

1. $\begin{vmatrix} i & j & k \\ 0 & 1 & 3 \\ 2 & -1 & 1 \end{vmatrix} = \begin{pmatrix} 4 \\ 6 \\ -2 \end{pmatrix}$ (Check before moving on that the answer is perpendicular to **a** and **b** using the scalar product.)

2. $C \to D = \mathbf{d} - \mathbf{c} = \begin{pmatrix} 4 \\ -2 \\ -7 \end{pmatrix} \Rightarrow \dfrac{x-2}{4} = \dfrac{y-1}{-2} = \dfrac{z-3}{-7}.$

3. $\begin{pmatrix} 2 \\ 1 \\ -2 \end{pmatrix} \cdot \begin{pmatrix} x \\ y \\ z \end{pmatrix} = \begin{pmatrix} 2 \\ 1 \\ -2 \end{pmatrix} \cdot \begin{pmatrix} 2 \\ -1 \\ 4 \end{pmatrix} = 4 - 1 - 8 = -5 \Rightarrow 2x + y - 2z + 5 = 0.$

4.   (a) $3P - 2Q = \begin{pmatrix} 6 & 3 \\ 9 & 12 \end{pmatrix} - \begin{pmatrix} 6 & 4 \\ -12 & 14 \end{pmatrix} = \begin{bmatrix} 0 & -1 \\ 21 & -2 \end{bmatrix}$

     (b) $PQ = \begin{pmatrix} 2 & 1 \\ 3 & 4 \end{pmatrix} \begin{pmatrix} 3 & 2 \\ -6 & 7 \end{pmatrix} = \begin{bmatrix} 0 & 11 \\ -15 & 34 \end{bmatrix}$

     (c) $R^{-1} = \dfrac{1}{4}\begin{pmatrix} 2 & -6 \\ -1 & 5 \end{pmatrix}$

     (d) $|S| = 2(-1-6) - 1(-4-4) + 3(12-2) = -14 + 8 + 30 = 24.$

5. $f(x) = e^{3x}$ $f(0) = 1$

     $f'(x) = 3e^{3x}$ $f'(0) = 3$

     $f''(x) = 9e^{3x}$ $f''(0) = 9$

     $f'''(x) = 27e^{3x}$ $f'''(0) = 27$ $f(x) = f(0) + xf'(0) + \dfrac{x^2}{2!}f''(0) + \dfrac{x^3}{3!}f'''(0) + \ldots\ldots$

     $\Rightarrow e^{3x} = 1 + x.3 + \dfrac{x^2}{2!}9 + \dfrac{x^3}{3!}27 + \ldots\ldots\ldots$

         $= 1 + 3x + \dfrac{9}{2}x^2 + \dfrac{9}{2}x^3 + \ldots\ldots\ldots .$

6.   2, 1·709, 1·604, 1·562, 1·544, 1·537, 1·534, 1·533, 1·532, 1·5325, 1·5322 $\Rightarrow$ 1·53

     (Always calculate sufficient guard figures after the degree of accuracy required in the answer.)

7. This is a linear first order differential equation, which can be solved using an integrating factor.

$$y' + Py = Q \quad \text{here } P = \frac{1}{x} \quad \int Pdx = \int \frac{1}{x} \, dx = \ln x \quad \Rightarrow \quad \text{integrating factor} = e^{\int Pdx} = e^{\ln x} = x.$$

Multiply through the equation by the integrating factor.

$$\Rightarrow x\frac{dy}{dx} + 1 \cdot y = x \sin x \quad \text{Note: the l.h.s. is always the derivative of (the integrating factor} \times y).$$

i.e. $\dfrac{d}{dx}(xy) = x \sin x$

$$\Rightarrow xy = \int x \sin x \, dx = \int x \, D(-\cos x) \, dx = -x \cos x + \int \cos x \, dx$$

$$= -x \cos x + \sin x + c$$

$$\Rightarrow y = \frac{c}{x} + \frac{1}{x} \sin x - \cos x.$$

8. Prove: $\displaystyle\sum_{t=1}^{n} t = \frac{1}{2}n(n+1)$ .... $p(n)$ a proposition regarding n.

Proof: if $n = 1$, l.h.s. $= 1$, r.h.s. $= \dfrac{1}{2} \times 1 \times 2 = 1 = $ l.h.s. $\Rightarrow p(1)$

Suppose $p(k)$ for some $k \in N$, i.e. $\displaystyle\sum_{t=1}^{k} t = \frac{1}{2}k(k+1)$.

$$\therefore \sum_{t=1}^{k+1} t = \sum_{t=1}^{k} t + (k+1) = \frac{1}{2}k(k+1) + (k+1) = \frac{1}{2}(k+1)[k+2]$$

$$= \frac{1}{2}n(n+1) \text{ where } n = k+1 \Rightarrow p(n+1)$$

i.e. $p(1)$ and $(p(k) \Rightarrow p(k+1))$ hence $p(n) \ \forall \ n \in N$ (q.e.d.)

9.

$$
\begin{array}{r}
4 \\
518 \overline{)\, 1961} \\
2072 \\
\end{array}
$$

$$
\begin{array}{r}
5 \\
-111 \overline{)\, 518} \\
555 \\
\end{array}
$$

$$
\begin{array}{r}
3 \\
-37 \overline{)\, 111} \\
111 \\
\hline
0 \quad \Rightarrow \quad (1961, 518) = 37.
\end{array}
$$

UNIT 3 TEST 2
ANSWERS

1. $\begin{pmatrix} -3 \\ 5 \\ 19 \end{pmatrix}$.

2. $\dfrac{x - 5}{2} = \dfrac{y + 3}{5} = \dfrac{z - 4}{-5}$.

3. $3x + 2y - z = 0$

4. (a) $\begin{pmatrix} 0 & 14 \\ 1 & -3 \end{pmatrix}$ (b) $\begin{pmatrix} 14 & 4 \\ 7 & 13 \end{pmatrix}$ (c) $\dfrac{1}{2}\begin{pmatrix} 9 & -5 \\ -5 & 3 \end{pmatrix}$ (d) 10

5. $1 + 5x + \dfrac{25}{2} x^2 + \dfrac{125}{6} x^3 + \ \text{.........} \ .$

6. 2·46.

7. $y = \sin x + \dfrac{1}{x} \cos x + \dfrac{c}{x}.$

8. The proof is almost identical to the last test but assume $p(r)$ and prove $p(r + 1)$.

9. 23.

Solutions and Answers

PRACTICE PRELIM PAPER 1
SOLUTIONS

1.   (a) $D(\cos x \sin^{-1} x) = \cos x \dfrac{1}{\sqrt{1 - x^2}} + (-\sin x)\sin^{-1} x = \dfrac{\cos x}{\sqrt{1 - x^2}} - \sin x \sin^{-1} x$

    (b) $D\left(\dfrac{3x + 2}{x^2 + 1}\right) = \dfrac{(x^2 + 1)(3) - (3x + 2)(2x)}{(x^2 + 1)^2} = \dfrac{3x^2 + 3 - 6x^2 - 4x}{(x^2 + 1)^2} = \dfrac{3 - 4x - 3x^2}{(x^2 + 1)^2}$

    (c) $D(e^{\sin^2 x}) = e^{\sin^2 x} D(\sin^2 x) = e^{\sin^2 x}\, 2\sin x \cos x = \sin2 x\, e^{\sin^2 x}.$

2.   (a) $e^{6x^2 + 3} + c$ (note that $12x$ is the derivative of $6x^2 + 3$)

    (b) $\ln(x^3 + 5x^2 + 11) + c$ (note that $3x^2 + 10x$ is the derivative of $x^3 + 5x^2 + 11$).

3.   (a)   a translation 1 to the right and 1 down, or in vector terms $\begin{pmatrix} 1 \\ -1 \end{pmatrix}$

    (b)   a spiral similarity, enlargement scale factor 2 and rotation of $+90°$

    (c)   a half turn about $(2, 0)$ [$(2, 0)$ is the mid-point of $(x + iy)$ and $(4 - x - iy)$].

4. $T_{r+1} = {}^9C_r(3x^2)^{9-r}\left(\dfrac{2}{x}\right)^r = {}^9C_r(3)^{9-r}(2)^r\, x^{18 - 2r - r}$

    for x^0, $18 - 3r = 0 \Rightarrow r = 6 \Rightarrow T_7 = \dfrac{9!}{6!\,3!}\, 3^3\, 2^6 = \dfrac{9 \times 8 \times 7}{3 \times 2} \times 3^3 \times 2^6 = 2^8 \times 3^4 \times 7 = 145\,152.$

5. $w = z_1 z_2 = 2 \times 3(\cos(30 + 60)° + i \sin(30 + 60)°) = 6(\cos 90° + i \sin 90°).$

6. $y = x \ln x \Rightarrow y' = x\dfrac{1}{x} + \ln x = 1 + \ln x$

    $x = e \Rightarrow \begin{cases} y = e \ln e = e \\[2mm] y' = 1 + \ln e = 2 \end{cases}$

    the line through (e, e) with gradient 2 is $y - e = 2(x - e)$
                                         $\Rightarrow y = 2x - e.$

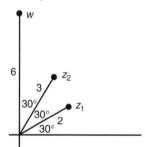

7. $\dfrac{dy}{dx} = \dfrac{x^2}{y} \Rightarrow y\, dy = x^2\, dx \Rightarrow \int y\, dy = \int x^2\, dx$

                                   $\Rightarrow \dfrac{y^2}{2} = \dfrac{x^3}{3} + c$

    $\left.\begin{matrix} x = 0 \\ y = 2 \end{matrix}\right\} \Rightarrow 2 = c \;\Rightarrow\; y^2 = \dfrac{2}{3}x^3 + 4.$

53

8. Prove: $\displaystyle\sum_{r=1}^{n} (2r - 1) = n^2$ .... $p(n)$ (a proposition concerning n.)

Proof: if $n = 1$, l.h.s. $= 1$, r.h.s. $= 1 = $ l.h.s. $\Rightarrow p(1)$

(The proposition concerning n is true when $n = 1$)

Suppose $p(k)$, i.e. $\displaystyle\sum_{r=1}^{k} (2r - 1) = k^2$

then $\displaystyle\sum_{r=1}^{k+1} (2r - 1) = \sum_{r=1}^{k} (2r - 1) + [2(k + 1) - 1] = k^2 + 2k + 1 = (k + 1)^2 = n^2$ where

$n = k + 1$, i.e. $p(k+1)$

Thus $p(1)$ and $p(k) \Rightarrow p(k + 1)$, hence $p(n) \ \forall \ n \in$ N.

9. $V = \displaystyle\int_{3}^{0} \pi y^2 \, dx = \pi \int_{3}^{0} \frac{1}{4} x^2 \, dx = \pi \left[\frac{x^3}{12}\right]_{3}^{0} = \frac{\pi}{12} [27 - 0] = \frac{9\pi}{4} \ units^3.$

10. (a) Let $\dfrac{2x + 1}{x^2 + x - 6} \equiv \dfrac{2x + 1}{(x - 2)(x + 3)} \equiv \dfrac{A}{x - 2} + \dfrac{B}{x + 3}$

$\therefore 2x + 1 \equiv A(x + 3) + B(x - 2)$

$x = 2 \ \Rightarrow \ 5 = 5A \ \Rightarrow \ A = 1$

$x = -3 \ \Rightarrow \ -5 = -5B \ \Rightarrow \ B = 1$

$\Rightarrow \dfrac{2x + 1}{x^2 + x - 6} \equiv \dfrac{1}{x - 2} + \dfrac{1}{x + 3}$ [check: work backwards]

(b) $\dfrac{x^3 + x^2 - 4x + 1}{x^2 + x - 6} = \dfrac{x^3 + x^2 - 6x + 2x + 1}{x^2 + x - 6} = x + \dfrac{2x + 1}{x^2 + x - 6} = x + \dfrac{1}{x - 2} + \dfrac{1}{x + 3}$

Hint! Divide the leading terms in the top and bottom lines i.e. $x^3 \div x^2 = x$, therefore arrange the top line to begin with x times the bottom line i.e.

$(x^3 + x^2 - 4x + 1 = x(x^2 + x - 6) + (2x + 1))$

$\Rightarrow \displaystyle\int \dfrac{x^3 + x^2 - 4x + 1}{x^2 + x - 6} \, dx = \int \left(x + \dfrac{1}{x - 2} + \dfrac{1}{x + 3}\right) \, dx = \int x \, dx + \int \dfrac{1}{x - 2} \, dx + \int \dfrac{1}{x + 3} \, dx$

$= \dfrac{1}{2} x^2 + \ln(x - 2) + \ln(x + 3) + c = \dfrac{1}{2} x^2 + \ln(x^2 + x - 6) + c.$

11. First find the smallest multiple of 7 not less than 300, and the biggest not exceeding 800.

These multiples are, in arithmetic progression: 301, 308, 315, ...,798.

using $T_n = a + (n - 1) d$, $798 = 301 + (n - 1) \times 7 \Rightarrow n - 1 = 497 \div 7 = 71$, so $n = 72.$

using $S_n = \dfrac{n}{2} (a + l)$, $S_{72} = \dfrac{72}{2} (301 + 798) = 36 \times 1099 = 6 \times 6594 = 39 \ 564.$

12. The first line is just Mathematics at the Higher level :

$$4x^3 - 12x^2 + 15x - 7 = (x - 1)(4x^2 - 8x + 7)$$

$$\therefore x = 1, \frac{8 \pm \sqrt{64 - 4 \times 4 \times 7}}{8} = 1, 1 \pm \frac{1}{8} \times 4 \times \sqrt{3}i = 1, 1 \pm \frac{1}{2}\sqrt{3}i.$$

13. $\displaystyle\int \frac{2x + 3}{x^2 + 4x + 8} \, dx = \int \frac{2x + 4 - 1}{x^2 + 4x + 8} \, dx = \int \frac{2x + 4}{x^2 + 4x + 8} \, dx - \int \frac{1}{(x + 2)^2 + 4} \, dx$

$$= \ln(x^2 + 4x + 8) - \frac{1}{2} \tan^{-1}\left(\frac{x + 2}{2}\right) + c.$$

14. (a) $u^2 = x^3 + 3$

$$\Rightarrow 2u \, du = 3x^2 \, dx \quad \therefore \int x^2 \sqrt{x^3 + 3} \, dx = \int \frac{2}{3} u \, u \, du = \frac{2}{3} \frac{u^3}{3} = \frac{2}{9}(x^3 + 3)^{3/2} + c.$$

(b) $\displaystyle\int x^2 \ln x \, dx = \int \ln x \, D\left(\frac{x^3}{3}\right) dx = \frac{1}{3} x^3 \ln x - \frac{1}{3}\int x^3 \frac{1}{x} \, dx = \frac{1}{3} x^3 \ln x - \frac{1}{3}\frac{x^3}{3} + c$

$$= \frac{1}{9} x^3 [\ln x^3 - 1] + c.$$

15. (a) Let $\displaystyle\frac{4(r + 1)}{r^2 (r + 2)^2} \equiv \frac{A}{r} + \frac{B}{r^2} + \frac{C}{r + 2} + \frac{D}{(r + 2)^2}$

$$\Rightarrow 4r + 4 \equiv Ar (r + 2)^2 + B (r + 2)^2 + Cr^2 (r + 2) + Dr^2$$

$r = 0 \quad \Rightarrow \quad 4 = 4B \quad \Rightarrow \quad B = 1$

$r = -2 \quad \Rightarrow \quad -4 = 4D \quad \Rightarrow \quad D = -1$

coeff. of $r \quad 4 = 4A + 4B = 4A + 4 \Rightarrow A = 0$

coeff. of $r^3 \quad 0 = A + C \Rightarrow C = 0$

$$\Rightarrow \frac{4(r + 1)}{r^2(r + 2)^2} \equiv \frac{1}{r^2} - \frac{1}{(r + 2)^2} \quad .$$

(b) $\displaystyle\sum_{r=1}^{n} \frac{4(r + 1)}{r^2(r + 2)^2} = \sum_{r=1}^{n} \left(\frac{1}{r^2} - \frac{1}{(r + 2)^2}\right) = \left(\frac{1}{1^2} - \frac{1}{3^2}\right) + \left(\frac{1}{2^2} - \frac{1}{4^2}\right) + \left(\frac{1}{3^2} - \frac{1}{5^2}\right)$

$$+ \left(\frac{1}{4^2} - \frac{1}{6^2}\right) + ... + \left(\frac{1}{(n - 2)^2} - \frac{1}{(n)^2}\right) + \left(\frac{1}{(n - 1)^2} - \frac{1}{(n + 1)^2}\right) + \left(\frac{1}{n^2} - \frac{1}{(n + 2)^2}\right)$$

$$= 1 + \frac{1}{4} - \frac{1}{(n + 1)^2} - \frac{1}{(n + 2)^2} = \frac{5}{4} - \frac{1}{(n + 1)^2} - \frac{1}{(n + 2)^2} \quad .$$

(c) $\displaystyle\sum_{r=1}^{\infty} \frac{4(r + 1)}{r^2(r + 2)^2} = \frac{5}{4} .$

16. (a) $|z| = \sqrt{16 + 48} = \sqrt{64} = 8$

$amp\,(z) = \theta = \tan^{-1}\left(\dfrac{4\sqrt{3}}{4}\right) = \dfrac{\pi}{3}$

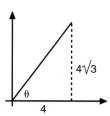

(b) $z = 8\left(\cos\left(\dfrac{\pi}{3}\right) + i\sin\left(\dfrac{\pi}{3}\right)\right) = 8\left[\cos\left(\dfrac{\pi}{3} + 2n\pi\right) + i\sin\left((6n + 1)\,\dfrac{\pi}{3}\right)\right]$

$\Rightarrow z^{\frac{1}{3}} = 2\left[\cos\left(\dfrac{\pi}{9} + \dfrac{2n\pi}{3}\right) + i\sin\left((6n + 1)\,\dfrac{\pi}{9}\right)\right]\quad n = 0,\,1,\,2$

Hence $z_1 = 2\left(\cos\dfrac{\pi}{9} + i\sin\dfrac{\pi}{9}\right)$,

$\Rightarrow \qquad z_2 = 2\left(\cos\dfrac{7\pi}{9} + i\sin\dfrac{7\pi}{9}\right)$,

$z_3 = 2\left(\cos\dfrac{13\pi}{9} + i\sin\dfrac{13\pi}{9}\right) = 2\left(\cos\dfrac{-5\pi}{9} + i\sin\dfrac{-5\pi}{9}\right).$

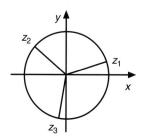

17. (a) $0 < \theta < \dfrac{2\pi}{3}$.

(b) $\dfrac{AC}{\sin\theta} = \dfrac{30}{\sin\dfrac{\pi}{3}} = \dfrac{30}{\sqrt{\dfrac{3}{2}}} = \dfrac{60}{\sqrt{3}} = 20\sqrt{3} \quad\Rightarrow\quad AC = 20\sqrt{3}\sin\theta$

Area $= \dfrac{1}{2}\,AC\,BC\,\sin\hat{C} = \dfrac{1}{2}\,20\sqrt{3}\sin\theta.\,30\sin(\pi - \hat{C}) = 300\sqrt{3}\sin\theta\sin\left(\dfrac{\pi}{3} + \theta\right).$

(c) $A'(\theta) = 300\sqrt{3}\left[\sin\theta\cos\left(\dfrac{\pi}{3} + \theta\right) + \cos\theta\sin\left(\dfrac{\pi}{3} + \theta\right)\right] = 300\sqrt{3}\sin\left(2\theta + \dfrac{\pi}{3}\right).$

$A''(\theta) = 300\sqrt{3}\cos\left(2\theta + \dfrac{\pi}{3}\right)2 = 600\sqrt{3}\cos\left(2\theta + \dfrac{\pi}{3}\right).$

for stationary points $A' = 0 \Rightarrow 2\theta + \dfrac{\pi}{3} = \pi,\,2\pi, \quad\Rightarrow\quad 2\theta = \dfrac{2\pi}{3},\dfrac{5\pi}{3} \quad\Rightarrow\quad \theta = \dfrac{\pi}{3},\dfrac{5\pi}{6},$

but $\dfrac{5\pi}{6} \notin \left(0,\dfrac{2\pi}{3}\right)$, so $\theta = \dfrac{\pi}{3}.$

$A''\left(\dfrac{\pi}{3}\right) = 600\sqrt{3}\cos\pi = -600\sqrt{3} < 0 \quad\Rightarrow\quad$ maximum turning point, hence greatest area.

18. (a) if $y = x$, then $3 + \dfrac{4}{t} = 4 + \dfrac{3}{t^2}$ i.e. $4t = t^2 + 3 \Rightarrow t^2 - 4t + 3 = 0 = (t - 1)(t - 3)$

$\therefore t = 1, 3 \Rightarrow (7, 7)$ and $(1\frac{3}{5}, 1\frac{2}{3})$.

(b) $\dfrac{dx}{dt} = -\dfrac{4}{t^2}, \quad \dfrac{dy}{dt} = -\dfrac{6}{t^3}, \quad \dfrac{dy}{dx} = \dfrac{dy}{dt}\dfrac{dt}{dx} = \dfrac{dy}{dt} \div \dfrac{dx}{dt} = -\dfrac{6}{t^3} \times -\dfrac{t^2}{4} = \dfrac{3}{2t}$

$t = 1 \quad (7,7) \quad \text{gradient} = \dfrac{3}{2} \Rightarrow y - 7 = \dfrac{3}{2}(x - 7) \Rightarrow 2y - 14 = 3x - 21$

$$\Rightarrow 2y = 3x - 7.$$

$t = 3 \quad (1\frac{3}{5}, 1\frac{2}{3}) \text{ gradient} = \dfrac{1}{2} \qquad \Rightarrow y - \dfrac{13}{3} = \dfrac{1}{2}\left(x - \dfrac{13}{3}\right) \Rightarrow 6y - 26 = 3x - 13$

$$\Rightarrow 6y = 3x + 13.$$

Solving $2y + 7 = 6y - 13 \Rightarrow 4y = 20 \Rightarrow y = 5 \Rightarrow x = \dfrac{17}{3}$

i.e. the tangents meet at $\left(\dfrac{17}{3}, 5\right)$.

(c) $\dfrac{d^2y}{dx^2} = \dfrac{d}{dx}\left(\dfrac{dy}{dx}\right) = \dfrac{d}{dt}\left(\dfrac{3}{2}t^{-1}\right)\dfrac{dt}{dx} = -\dfrac{3}{2}\dfrac{1}{t^2}\dfrac{t^2}{-4} = \dfrac{3}{8}$

i.e. y'' is constant, so y' is linear, so y is quadratic.

also $y'' > 0 \Rightarrow$ 'concave up', hence a parabola with a minimum turning point.

PRACTICE PRELIM PAPER 2
ANSWERS

1. $(x, y, z) = (9, -2, 4)$.

2. (a) $\dfrac{\sec^2 x}{\tan x} = 2\operatorname{cosec} 2x$ (b) $e^x(\sin x + \cos x)$ (c) $\dfrac{2}{1 - x^2}$.

3. (a) $6 + \ln 8$ (b) $\dfrac{2}{3}\sqrt{3} - \dfrac{\pi}{6}$.

4. (a) reflection in $y = x$ (b) spiral similarity, enlarge scale factor 3, rotate $+ 30°$.

5. $2^4 \times 3^{10} \times 5 = 4\,723\,920$.

6. $-1 + i$.

7. Proof.
    [Hint : $k^2(k + 1) + (k + 1)(3k + 2) = (k + 1)\,[\ldots\ldots] = \ldots = (k + 1)^2\,(k + 2)$]

8. If $x = 0$, $y = 4$ in both cases. Gradients are $-\dfrac{1}{2}$ and 2, which have a product of -1.

9. 33 660.

10. $y = 4e^{\frac{x^2}{2} + 2x} - 1$.

11. (a) proof.   (b) $-2 \pm i$.

12. $y = 2x + 1$.

13. (a) $\dfrac{\pi}{4}$ (b) $\dfrac{x^4}{16}\,[\ln x^4 - 1] + c$.

14. (a) $(x - 2)(x^2 + 4x + 5)$ (b) $\Delta = -4 < 0$ (c) $\dfrac{2}{x - 2} + \dfrac{1 - 2x}{x^2 + 4x + 5}$

    (d) $2 \ln (x - 2) - \ln (x^2 + 4x + 5) + 5 \tan^{-1} (x + 2) + c$.

15. $\dfrac{dy}{dx} = \dfrac{(x - 1)(x - 3)}{(x - 2)^2}$, $\dfrac{d^2y}{dx^2} = \dfrac{2}{(x - 2)^3}$.   (1, 0) is a maximum turning point. (3, 4) is a minimum turning point.

16. (a) (i) $\dfrac{1}{2}n(n + 1)$ (ii) $\dfrac{1}{6}n(n + 1)(2n + 1)$

    (b) (i) $\dfrac{1}{3}n(n + 1)(n + 2)$ (ii) $\dfrac{1}{6}n(2n + 1)(7n + 1)$.

PRACTICE EXAM PAPER 1
SOLUTIONS

1.

$$
\begin{array}{ccc|c}
1 & 2 & -3 & 10 \\
2 & -3 & 4 & -4 \\
5 & -4 & 1 & 6 \\
\end{array}
$$

$$
\begin{array}{l}
r_2 - 2r_1 \\
r_3 - 5r_1 \\
r_5 - 2r_4
\end{array}
\quad
\begin{array}{ccc|c}
0 & -7 & 10 & -24 \\
0 & -14 & 16 & -44 \\
0 & 0 & -4 & 4
\end{array}
$$

$$
\begin{array}{ll}
\Rightarrow -4z = 4 & \Rightarrow z = -1 \\
r_4 \quad \Rightarrow 7y = 10z + 24 & \Rightarrow y = 2 \\
r_1 \quad \Rightarrow x = 10 - 4 - 3 & \Rightarrow x = 3 \\
\Rightarrow (x, y, z) = (3, 2, -1).
\end{array}
$$

2. $\left(x^3 - \dfrac{3}{x}\right)^5 = 1(x^3)^5 + 5(x^3)^4\left(-\dfrac{3}{x}\right) + 10(x^3)^3\left(-\dfrac{3}{x}\right)^2 + 10(x^3)^2\left(-\dfrac{3}{x}\right)^3 + 5(x^3)\left(-\dfrac{3}{x}\right)^4 + 1\left(-\dfrac{3}{x}\right)^5$

$$
= x^{15} - 15x^{11} + 90x^7 - 270x^3 + \frac{405}{x} - \frac{243}{x^5}.
$$

3. Let $\dfrac{(x + 2)^2}{x^2(x - 2)} \equiv \dfrac{A}{x} + \dfrac{B}{x^2} + \dfrac{C}{x - 2}$ so $x^2 + 4x + 4 \equiv Ax(x - 2) + B(x - 2) + Cx^2$

$$
\left.\begin{array}{lll}
x = 0 \Rightarrow & 4 = -2B & \Rightarrow B = -2 \\
x = 2 \Rightarrow & 16 = 4C & \Rightarrow C = 4 \\
\text{coeff. of } x^2: & 1 = A + C & \Rightarrow A = -3
\end{array}\right\}
\Rightarrow
\frac{4}{x - 2} - \frac{3}{x} - \frac{2}{x^2}.
$$

4. (a) $2xy + y^3 = 5 \Rightarrow 2xy' + 2y + 3y^2 y' = 0 \Rightarrow (2x + 3y^2)y' = -2y$

$$
\Rightarrow y' = \frac{-2y}{2x + 3y^2}.
$$

(b) $\therefore m_{(2,1)} = \dfrac{-2}{4 + 3} = -\dfrac{2}{7} \Rightarrow y - 1 = -\dfrac{2}{7}(x - 2) \Rightarrow 7y - 7 = -2x + 4$

i.e. $2x + 7y = 11.$

5. (a) $A^2 = \begin{bmatrix} 2 & -3 \\ 4 & 5 \end{bmatrix}\begin{bmatrix} 2 & -3 \\ 4 & 5 \end{bmatrix} = \begin{bmatrix} -8 & -21 \\ 28 & 13 \end{bmatrix}$ $\quad 7A - 22I = \begin{bmatrix} 14 & -21 \\ 28 & 35 \end{bmatrix} - \begin{bmatrix} 22 & 0 \\ 0 & 22 \end{bmatrix} = \begin{bmatrix} -8 & -21 \\ 28 & 13 \end{bmatrix}$

$\Rightarrow A^2 = 7A - 22I$ (q.e.d).

(b) (i) $A^2 = 7A - 22I \Rightarrow A^3 = A(7A - 22I) = 7A^2 - 22A = 7(7A - 22I) - 22A = 27A - 154I.$

(ii) $A^2 = 7A - 22I \Rightarrow A = 7I - 22A^{-1} \Rightarrow A^{-1} = \dfrac{1}{22}(7I - A).$

6. $\displaystyle\int x\sqrt{1 - x}\,dx = \int x\, D\left(-\frac{2}{3}(1 - x)^{\frac{3}{2}}\right)dx = -\frac{2}{3}x(1 - x)^{\frac{3}{2}} + \frac{2}{3}\int (1 - x)^{\frac{3}{2}}\,1\,dx$

$$
= -\frac{2}{3}x(1 - x)^{\frac{3}{2}} + \frac{2}{3}(1 - x)^{\frac{5}{2}}\frac{2}{5}(-1) + c
$$

$$
= c - \frac{2}{3}x(1 - x)^{\frac{3}{2}} - \frac{4}{15}(1 - x)^{\frac{5}{2}}.
$$

7. $u = 1 + \sin x$ $x = \dfrac{\pi}{2}$ $\Rightarrow u = \dfrac{3}{2}$

$\Rightarrow du = \cos x \, dx$ $x = \dfrac{\pi}{2}$ $\Rightarrow u = 2$

$$\therefore \int_{\frac{\pi}{6}}^{\frac{\pi}{2}} \frac{\cos x \, dx}{1 + \sin x} = \int_{\frac{3}{2}}^{2} \frac{du}{u} = \Big[\ln u\Big]_{\frac{3}{2}}^{2} = \ln 2 - \ln \frac{3}{2} = \ln \frac{2}{\frac{3}{2}} = \ln \frac{4}{3}.$$

8.   (Proof)   Let $5^n + 4n + 7 = f(n)$
so $f(1) = 5 + 4 + 7 = 16 = 4 \times 4 \Rightarrow 4|f(1)$
Suppose $4|f(k)$ for some $k \in N$
i.e. $f(k) = 4a$ for some a in $\mathbf{Z}$
Then $f(k + 1) - f(k) = [5^{k+1} + 4k + 4 + 7] - [5^k + 4k + 7]$
$\qquad\qquad\qquad\qquad = 5^k (5 - 1) + 4 = 4[5^k + 1]$
$\qquad\qquad\qquad\qquad = 4\beta$ where $\beta = 5^k + 1$
Hence $f(k + 1) = f(k) + 4\beta = 4a + 4\beta = 4(a + \beta)$
$\Rightarrow 4|f(k + 1)$
i.e. $4|f(1)$ and $[4|f(k) \Rightarrow 4|f(k + 1)]$
Hence $4|f(n)$ for all $n \in N$.

9. $y = \dfrac{x - 1}{e^x} \Rightarrow y' = \dfrac{e^x (1) - (x - 1)e^x}{(e^x)^2} = \dfrac{e^x}{(e^x)^2}[1 - x + 1] = \dfrac{2 - x}{e^x} = 0$ for stationary points

$\Rightarrow x = 2 \Rightarrow y = \dfrac{1}{e^2} \Rightarrow \left(2, \dfrac{1}{e^2}\right)$ is the stationary point.

$y'' = \dfrac{e^x(-1) - (2 - x)e^x}{(e^x)^2} = \dfrac{x - 3}{e^x} \Rightarrow y''(2) = -\dfrac{1}{e^2} < 0$

$\Rightarrow$ maximum turning value $= \dfrac{1}{e^2}$

For points of inflexion $y'' = 0$ $\Rightarrow x = 3 \Rightarrow y = \dfrac{2}{e^3} \Rightarrow \left(3, \dfrac{2}{e^3}\right)$ is the point of inflexion.

10. $z^3 = 8 = 8(\cos 2k\pi \pm i \sin 2k\pi)$ $\Rightarrow z = 2\left(\cos \dfrac{2k\pi}{3} \pm i \sin \dfrac{2k\pi}{3}\right), \; k = 0, 1$

$z_1 = 2 \quad z_{2,3} = 2\left(\cos \dfrac{2\pi}{3} \pm i \sin \dfrac{2\pi}{3}\right)$

i.e. $z \in \{2, \quad 2\left(\cos \dfrac{2\pi}{3} \pm i \sin \dfrac{2\pi}{3}\right)\}$.

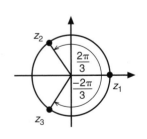

11. $f(x) = \sec x$ $\hfill f(0) = 1$

$f'(x) = \sec x \tan x$ $\hfill f'(0) = 0$

$f''(x) = \sec x \sec^2 x + \sec x \tan x \tan x = \sec x \,[\sec^2 x + \tan^2 x]$

$\qquad = \sec x \,[1 + 2 \tan^2 x]$ $\hfill f''(0) = 1$

$f'''(x) = \sec x \,[4 \tan x \sec^2 x] + \sec x \tan x \,[1 + 2 \tan^2 x]$

$\qquad = \sec x \tan x \,[4 \sec^2 x + 1 + 2 \tan^2 x] = \sec x \tan x \,[5 + 6 \tan^2 x]$

$\qquad = \sec x \,[5 \tan x + 6 \tan^3 x]$ $\hfill f'''(0) = 0$

$f^{(\mathrm{iv})}(x) = \sec x \,[5 \sec^2 x + 18 \tan^2 x \sec^2 x] + \sec x \tan x \,[5 \tan x + 6 \tan^3 x]$ $\hfill f^{(\mathrm{iv})}(0) = 5$

$f(x) = f(0) + f'(0)\, x + f''(0) \dfrac{x^2}{2!} + f'''(0) \dfrac{x^3}{3!} + f^{(\mathrm{iv})}(0) \dfrac{x^4}{4!} + \ldots\ldots$

$\Rightarrow \sec x = 1 + 0 + 1\dfrac{x^2}{2} + 0 + 5\dfrac{x^4}{24} + \ldots\ldots\ldots$

$\qquad = 1 + \dfrac{1}{2} x^2 + \dfrac{5}{24} x^4 + \ldots\ldots\ldots$

12. $\dfrac{dy}{dx} = \dfrac{y - y^2}{x^2} \quad\Rightarrow\quad \dfrac{dy}{y - y^2} = \dfrac{dx}{x^2} \quad\Rightarrow\quad \displaystyle\int \dfrac{dy}{y(1 - y)} = \int \dfrac{dx}{x^2}.$

Let $\dfrac{1}{y(1 - y)} \equiv \dfrac{A}{y} + \dfrac{B}{1 - y} \quad so \quad 1 \equiv A(1 - y) + By \quad \therefore A = B = 1$

$\Rightarrow \dfrac{1}{y} + \dfrac{1}{1 - y}$

$\Rightarrow \displaystyle\int \left(\dfrac{1}{y} + \dfrac{1}{1 - y}\right) dy = \dfrac{x^{-1}}{-1} + c$

$\Rightarrow \ln y - \ln (1 - y) = \ln\!\left(\dfrac{y}{1 - y}\right) = c - \dfrac{1}{x}$

$\Rightarrow \dfrac{y}{1 - y} = e^{c - \frac{1}{x}} = e^c e^{-\frac{1}{x}} = A e^{-\frac{1}{x}}$

$\Rightarrow y = A e^{-\frac{1}{x}} - y A e^{-\frac{1}{x}} \quad\Rightarrow\quad y(1 + A e^{-\frac{1}{x}}) = A e^{-\frac{1}{x}} \quad\Rightarrow\quad y = \dfrac{A e^{-\frac{1}{x}}}{1 + A e^{-\frac{1}{x}}} = \dfrac{A}{A + e^{-\frac{1}{x}}}$

$= \dfrac{1}{1 + C\, e^{\frac{1}{x}}}.$

13. (a) $u_3 = a + 2d = 11$

$\qquad u_7 = a + 6d = 23 \quad\Rightarrow 4d = 12 \qquad\Rightarrow d = 3 \qquad\Rightarrow a = 5$

$\qquad\qquad\qquad\qquad\qquad \Rightarrow u_6 = a + 5d = 5 + 15 = 20$

$\qquad\qquad\qquad\qquad\qquad u_{10} = a + 9d = 5 + 27 = 32.$

(b) $r = \dfrac{v_2}{v_1} = \dfrac{u_6}{u_{10}} = \dfrac{20}{32} = \dfrac{5}{8} \quad\Rightarrow\quad S_\infty = \dfrac{a}{1 - r} = \dfrac{32}{1 - \dfrac{5}{8}} = \dfrac{32}{\dfrac{3}{8}} = \dfrac{256}{3} = 85\dfrac{1}{3}.$

(c) $32\left(\dfrac{5}{8}\right)^{n-1}$

14. (a) $x = 0 \Rightarrow t = \dfrac{1}{2}$ $\Rightarrow \left(0, -\dfrac{7}{8}\right)$

   $y = 0 \Rightarrow t = 1$ $\Rightarrow (7, 0)$ i.e. one point on each axis.

(b) $\dfrac{dx}{dt} = \dfrac{3}{t^4},\ \dfrac{dy}{dt} = 3t^2$ $\Rightarrow$ $\dfrac{dy}{dx} = \dfrac{dy}{dt}\dfrac{dt}{dx} = \dfrac{dy}{dt} \div \dfrac{dx}{dt} = \dfrac{3t^2}{\dfrac{3}{t^4}} = t^6$

   $t = 1 \Rightarrow m = 1$ at $(7, 0)$ $\Rightarrow y - 0 = 1(x - 7)$ $\Rightarrow y = x - 7$

   $t = \dfrac{1}{2} \Rightarrow m = \dfrac{1}{64}$ at $\left(0, -\dfrac{7}{8}\right)$ $\Rightarrow y + \dfrac{7}{8} = \dfrac{1}{64}(x - 0)$ $\Rightarrow 64y + 56 = x$

   solving: $y + 7 = x = 64y + 56 \Rightarrow 0 = 63y + 49$ $\Rightarrow y = -\dfrac{7}{9}$ $\Rightarrow$ $x = 7 - \dfrac{7}{9} = \dfrac{56}{9}$

   $\Rightarrow x + 8y = \dfrac{56}{9} + 8\left(-\dfrac{7}{9}\right) = 0 \Rightarrow$ the pt. of intersection of the tangents lies on $x + 8y = 0$.

(c) $\dfrac{d^2y}{dx^2} = \dfrac{d}{dx}\left(\dfrac{dy}{dx}\right) = \dfrac{d}{dt}(t^6)\dfrac{dt}{dx} = 6t^5\,\dfrac{t^4}{3} = 2t^9 = 0$ for points of inflexion $\Rightarrow t = 0$.

   But $t \neq 0$, so there are no points of inflexion.

15. (a) $\dfrac{dy}{dx} + \dfrac{y}{x} = x^2$ is linear, i.e. of the form $y' + P(x)\,y = Q(x)$ with 'P' $= \dfrac{1}{x}$.

   $\displaystyle\int P dx = \int \dfrac{1}{x}\, dx = \ln x \Rightarrow$ integrating factor $= e^{\ln x} = x$

   $\Rightarrow x\,y' + y = x^3$ $\Rightarrow$ $\dfrac{d}{dx}(xy) = x^3$ $\Rightarrow$ $xy = \dfrac{x^4}{4} + c$ $\Rightarrow$ $y = \dfrac{c}{x} + \dfrac{1}{4}x^3$

(b) $x = 4, y = 20$ $\Rightarrow$ $20 = \dfrac{c}{4} + 16$ $\Rightarrow$ $c = 16$ $\Rightarrow$ $y = \dfrac{16}{x} + \dfrac{1}{4}x^3$.

(c)   Try $y = Ae^{mx}$ $y'' - 4y' + 13y = 0$
   so $y' = Ae^{mx}\, m = my$ $\Rightarrow m^2 y - 4my + 13y = 0$
   $y'' = my' = m^2 y$ $\Rightarrow m^2 - 4m + 13 = 0$

   $\Rightarrow m = \dfrac{4 \pm \sqrt{16 - 4 \times 1 \times 13}}{2} = \dfrac{4 \pm \sqrt{-36}}{2} = 2 \pm 3i$

   $\Rightarrow y = e^{2x}(A\cos 3x + B\sin 3x)$

16. (*a*) $\overrightarrow{BA} = \begin{pmatrix} 3 \\ -2 \\ 16 \end{pmatrix}$ $\overrightarrow{CA} = \begin{pmatrix} 1 \\ -1 \\ 5 \end{pmatrix}$ $\mathbf{n}_1 = \begin{vmatrix} i & j & k \\ 3 & -2 & 16 \\ 1 & -1 & 5 \end{vmatrix} = \begin{pmatrix} 6 \\ 1 \\ -1 \end{pmatrix}$ (check using the dot product)

$$\Rightarrow \begin{pmatrix} 6 \\ 1 \\ -1 \end{pmatrix} \cdot \begin{pmatrix} x \\ y \\ z \end{pmatrix} = \begin{pmatrix} 6 \\ 1 \\ -1 \end{pmatrix} \cdot \begin{pmatrix} 1 \\ 2 \\ 10 \end{pmatrix} = 6 + 2 - 10 = -2 \Rightarrow 6x + y - z + 2 = 0.$$

(*b*) $\mathbf{n}_2 = \begin{pmatrix} 2 \\ -1 \\ 3 \end{pmatrix} \Rightarrow \mathbf{u} = \mathbf{n}_1 \times \mathbf{n}_2 = \begin{vmatrix} i & j & k \\ 6 & 1 & -1 \\ 2 & -1 & 3 \end{vmatrix} = \begin{pmatrix} 2 \\ -20 \\ -8 \end{pmatrix} = 2 \begin{pmatrix} 1 \\ -10 \\ -4 \end{pmatrix}.$

For a point on the line of intersection, let $x = 0$,

so $\begin{cases} y - z = -2 \\ -y + 3z = 16 \end{cases}$ $\Rightarrow$ $2z = 14$ $\Rightarrow$ $z = 7$ $\Rightarrow$ $y = z - 2 = 5$ $\Rightarrow$ $(0, 5, 7)$

hence $\dfrac{x}{1} = \dfrac{y - 5}{-10} = \dfrac{z - 7}{-4}$.

(*c*) BB' is $\dfrac{x + 2}{2} = \dfrac{y - 4}{-1} = \dfrac{z + 6}{3} = t$

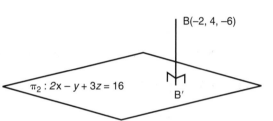

$\pi_2 : 2x - y + 3z = 16$ B(–2, 4, –6)   B′

so B' is of the form $(2t - 2, -t + 4, 3t - 6)$.
Substituting in π_2:
$2(2t - 2) - (-t + 4) + 3(3t - 6) = 16$
$\Rightarrow 14t = 42 \Rightarrow t = 3 \Rightarrow B'(4, 1, 3)$

PRACTICE EXAM PAPER 2
ANSWERS

1. $(x, y, z) = (3, -4, -1)$.

2. (a), (b) easy proofs.

3. (a) reflection in the x-axis $\quad(b)$ +ve quarter turn about O $\quad(c)$ half-turn about $(1, 0)$.

4. -120.

5. proof (remember to use the chain rule and quotient rule).

6. $2x^{\frac{1}{2}} + 4x^{\frac{1}{4}} + 4\ln\left(x^{\frac{1}{4}} - 1\right) + c$.

7. proof (after differentiating implicitly, multiply everything by $(x + y)$,
$(x + y)^3$ becomes $(x + y)^4$, for which $4xy$ can be substituted).

8. proof : let $f(n) = 4^n + 6n + 8$, show $9 \mid f(1)$, assume $9 \mid f(k)$, consider $f(k + 1) - f(k)$.

9. $(0, 0)$ is a rising point of inflexion $\qquad (-3, -27)$ is a minimum turning point.

$(-2, -16)$

$m = 16$

10. proof : use $\Sigma 1 = n$ and telescoping terms
i.e. $(2^2 - 1^2) + (3^2 - 2^2) + (4^2 - 3^2) + \ldots\ldots\ldots + (n + 1)^2 - n^2 = (n + 1)^2 - 1$.

11. $x - \dfrac{1}{2}x^2 + \dfrac{1}{6}x^3 - \dfrac{1}{12}x^4 + \ldots$.

12. (a) proof: factorise to $(n-1)n(n+1)$
$\quad(b)$ (i) true, prove using the contrapositive
$\qquad$ (ii) false, e.g. counter-example $6 \mid 72 \Rightarrow 6 \mid 8 \times 9$ but 6 does not divide 8 or 9.

13. (a) $\dfrac{dT}{dt} = k(T - a)$ $\quad(b)$ $T = a + Ae^{kt}$ $\quad(c)$ another 3 minutes 25 seconds (i.e. $t = 5 \cdot 419$).

14. $y = Ae^{2x} + Be^{5x} + x^2 + 2; \quad y = x^2 + 2 - 2e^{2x} + e^{5x}$.

15. (a) A $(-1, 3, -1)$ $\quad(b)$ proof : use $\mathbf{n} = \begin{pmatrix} 1 \\ 2 \\ 1 \end{pmatrix} \times \begin{pmatrix} 2 \\ -3 \\ -1 \end{pmatrix}$
$\quad(c)$ $\dfrac{x + 1}{17} = \dfrac{y - 3}{-8} = \dfrac{z + 1}{-1}$.

16. $\dfrac{1}{x + 3} - \dfrac{3}{x^2 + 9} \quad$ + proof (use standard integrals on these partial fractions).

64

PRACTICE EXAM PAPER 3
ANSWERS

1. $2^{-5} \times 3^5 \times 5 \times 7 = \dfrac{8505}{32}$.   **2.** $-\dfrac{\pi}{2}$.

3. $3x^2\,(x\sin 6x + \sin^2 3x)$ *or* $3x^2\sin 3x[2x\cos 3x + \sin 3x]$.

4.   (*a*)   (4, 1)   (*b*) $(-2, 4)$ small changes in coefficients produce disproportionate effects in the answer $\Rightarrow$ these sets of equations are ill-conditioned.

5.   Proof : differentiate x and y w.r.t. θ, then use the chain rule.   **6.**   (*a*) -15 (*b*) $\dfrac{9}{4}$.

7.   (*a*)   both equal $\begin{pmatrix} 43 & 54 \\ 27 & 34 \end{pmatrix}$.   (*b*)   multiply result (a) by A and use (a) again.   (*c*)   use (a) $\times A^{-1}$

8. $\dfrac{592\pi}{45}$ units^3.   **9.**   Proof : use $\displaystyle\sum_{r=1}^{k+1} \dfrac{1}{(3r-2)(3r+1)} = \dfrac{k}{3k+1} + \dfrac{1}{(3k+1)(3k+4)}$.

10.   (*a*) $5n(n + 19)$ (*b*)   13.   **11.** $\dfrac{3}{x} + \dfrac{4}{x^2} - \dfrac{3x+4}{x^2+1}$.

12.   (*a*) $f(1) < 0$, $f(2) > 0$ 1·9   (*b*)   1·902

13. $x = 49, y = -15$.

14.   (*a*)   both coordinate axes, as shown in complete sketch.

      (*b*)   maximum at $\left(\dfrac{3}{2}, \dfrac{16}{9}\right)$, minimum at $\left(-\dfrac{3}{2}, -\dfrac{16}{9}\right)$.

      (*c*)

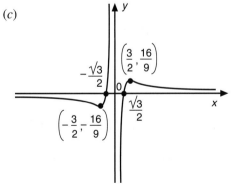

15.   (*a*)   proof : use Pascal's triangle and separate real and imaginary parts.
       (*b*) $(\cos 5\theta + i\sin 5\theta)$.
       (*c*)   (i) $\cos 5\theta = 16\cos^5\theta - 20\cos^3\theta + 5\cos\theta$ (ii) $\sin 5\theta = 16\sin^5\theta - 20\sin^3\theta + 5\sin\theta$.
       (*d*)   proof : use $\tan x = \sin x \div \cos x$, $1 \div \cos x = \sec x$ and $\sec^2 x = 1 + \tan^2 x$.

16.   (*a*) $y = 5e^{3x} + 2e^{-4x}$.

        (*b*) $y = \dfrac{1}{5}(x + 2)^2 + c(x + 2)^{-3}, \quad y = \dfrac{(x + 2)^5 + 4}{5(x + 2)^3}$.

17.   (*a*) $2x + y + 4z = 6$.

        (*b*) $\dfrac{x - 6}{-6} : \dfrac{y + 6}{8} = t$.

PRACTICE EXAM PAPER 4
ANSWERS

1. There are an infinite number of solutions of the form $(2 - t, 8t + 11, 5t + 3)$ not uniquely

i.e. all the points on the line with equations $\dfrac{x - 2}{-1} = \dfrac{y - 11}{8} = \dfrac{z - 3}{5}$.

2. $\dfrac{1}{x} + \dfrac{1}{x^2} + \dfrac{1}{x - 1}$.

3. (*a*) $x + \tan^{-1}\left(\dfrac{x}{2}\right) + \dfrac{3}{2}\ln(x^2 + 4) + c$ (*b*) $2x \sin^{-1} x + \dfrac{x^2}{\sqrt{1 - x^2}}$.

4. $5x + 4y = 14$ **5.** $y = \sin^{-1}(1 - \cos x)$.

6. (*a*) $\dfrac{z^5 - 1}{z - 1}$ (*b*) $\{1, (\cos\dfrac{2\pi}{5} \pm i \sin\dfrac{2\pi}{5}), (\cos\dfrac{4\pi}{5} \pm i \sin\dfrac{4\pi}{5})\}$

(*c*) $\left[z^2 - (2\cos\dfrac{2\pi}{5})z + 1\right]\left[z^2 - (2\cos\dfrac{4\pi}{5})z + 1\right]$.

7. $\begin{bmatrix} 2-\lambda & -2 & 0 \\ 1 & -\lambda & 2 \\ -2 & 2 & -\lambda \end{bmatrix}$, $0, 1 \pm \sqrt{3}$.

8. Proof : let $5^n + 12n - 1 = f(n)$, show $16 \,|\, f(1)$, assume $16 \,|\, f(k)$, consider $f(k + 1) - f(k)$.

9. $a < a^2 \Rightarrow a < a^3$ False. Any value of $a < -1$ is a counter-example.

10. $-x^2 - \dfrac{1}{6}x^4 - \dots$.

11. $x = 49$ $y = -53$.

12. (*a*) $x = 2$ and $y = 0$, as shown in complete sketch

(*b*) $\left(-2, -\dfrac{1}{2}\right)$ is a minimum turning point

(*c*)

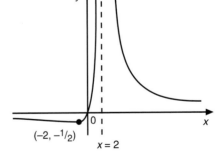

13. (*a*) $\dfrac{1}{r + 2} - \dfrac{1}{r + 3}$ (*b*) $\dfrac{n}{3(n + 3)}$ (*c*) $\dfrac{n}{(n + 3)(2n + 3)}$.

14. (*a*) $(4, 0, 2)$ (*b*) $x + 5y + 7z = 18$ (*c*) $-10.9°$.

15. (*a*) $y = (Ax + B)e^{3x} + e^{2x}$ (*b*) $y = (2x + 1)e^{3x} + e^{2x}$.

PRACTICE EXAM PAPER 5
ANSWERS

1. $\dfrac{1}{x} + \dfrac{2}{x^2} + \dfrac{3}{x-2}$.

2. (a) $k = 6$ (b) $A^{-1} = \dfrac{1}{6} B$.

3. $-\dfrac{6}{25}$.

4. $(-1, 5)$, $(7, -1)$, so ill-conditioned.

5. $2^8 \times 3^4 \times 7 = 145\,152$.

6. (a) proof : $v = \sqrt{\dot{x}^2 + \dot{y}^2}$ (b) $a = 1 =$ constant.

7. $1 \cdot 2\pi$ cm²/s $(3 \cdot 77)$.

8. Proof : use $\displaystyle\sum_{r=1}^{k+1} (-1)^r \dfrac{2r+1}{r(r+1)} = \left[\dfrac{(-1)^{k-1}}{k+1} + 1 \right] + \dfrac{(-1)^k (2k+3)}{(k+1)(k+2)}$.

9. 75 or 225.

10. $y = 2x\, e^{5x}$.

11. $4 - x^2 + \dfrac{1}{3} x^3 + \,.....\,$.

12. (a) proof : use $a = 2x + 1$, $b = 2y + 1$

    (b) converse : $a^2 + b^2$ divisible by 2 but not by 4 $\Rightarrow a, b$ are odd

    True : prove using the contrapositive.

13. $y = c \sin x + \sin^2 x - x \cos x \sin x$.

14. (a) $A = \dfrac{1}{4} \cos \theta\, (2 + \sin \theta)$

    (b) proof : use $A'(\theta) = -\dfrac{1}{4} [2\sin^2\theta + 2\sin\theta - 1]$ $A''(\theta) = -\dfrac{1}{2} \cos \theta\, (2\sin\theta + 1)$

    (c) proof : use Pythagoras' Theorem to find $\cos \theta$.

15. (a) proof : separate the variables and use partial fractions, integrate, make p the subject

    (b) $k = \dfrac{1}{100} \ln \dfrac{27}{17} \cong 0 \cdot 00463$.

16. $z \in \{1 \pm i, -1 \pm i\}$.

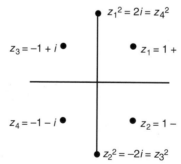

17. (a) AB : $\dfrac{x - 12}{8} = \dfrac{y - 5}{1} = \dfrac{z + 2}{-4}$ CD : $\dfrac{x + 1}{1} = \dfrac{y + 6}{2} = \dfrac{z + 3}{1}$

    (b) $(4, 4, 2)$

    (c) $3x - 4y + 5z = 6$.

PRACTICE EXAM PAPER 6
ANSWERS

1. none. **2.** 196. **3.** $\dfrac{\cos x - \sin x - 1}{3 - 2\cos x + 2\sin x}$.

4. $c - \sin^{-1}\dfrac{x}{3} - 2\sqrt{9 - x^2}$. **5.** $y = \cos 5x + e^{5x}(F\cos 2x + G\sin 2x)$.

6. $y = Ae^{2\tan^{-1}x}$, $y = 3e^{2\tan^{-1}x}$. **7.** (a) $\begin{bmatrix} 0 & -1 \\ -1 & 0 \end{bmatrix}$. (b) $(-1, -2)$

8. $\dfrac{1 + \sin x - \cos x}{(1 + \sin x)^2}$. **9.** Proof : use $\sum\limits_{r=1}^{k+1}(6r + 1) = k(3k + 4) + (6k + 7)$.

10. (a) $f'(x) = \left(\dfrac{x - 1}{x^2}\right)e^x$, $f''(x) = \left(\dfrac{x^2 - 2x + 2}{x^3}\right)e^x$

  (b) when $x = 1$, e is the minimum turning value.

11. $p = -1, q = 4$.

12. $(3a)^3 + 3(3a)^2\left(\dfrac{-4}{b}\right) + 3(3a)\left(\dfrac{-4}{b}\right)^2 + \left(\dfrac{-4}{b}\right)^3$

  $= 27a^3 - \dfrac{108a^2}{b} + \dfrac{144a}{b^2} - \dfrac{64}{b^3}$

13. (a) $e^x = 1 + x + \dfrac{x^2}{2} + \dfrac{x^3}{6}$

  (b) $e^{x^3} = 1 + x^3$

  (c) $e^{x + x^3} = \left(1 + x + \dfrac{x^2}{2} + \dfrac{x^3}{6}\right)(1 + x^3)$

   $= 1 + x + \dfrac{x^2}{2} + \dfrac{x^3}{6} + x^3$

   $= 1 + x + \dfrac{x^2}{2} + \dfrac{7x^3}{6}$

14. (a) $2^{\frac{1}{4}}\left(\cos\dfrac{5\pi}{24} + i\sin\dfrac{5\pi}{24}\right)$, $2^{\frac{1}{4}}\left(\cos\dfrac{17\pi}{24} + i\sin\dfrac{17\pi}{24}\right)$,

   $2^{\frac{1}{4}}\left(\cos\dfrac{-19\pi}{24} + i\sin\dfrac{-19\pi}{24}\right)$, $2^{\frac{1}{4}}\left(\cos\dfrac{-7\pi}{24} + i\sin\dfrac{-7\pi}{24}\right)$

  (b) $|z| = 5$ amp$(z) = -143 \cdot 1°$.

15. (a) $\dfrac{1}{r + 3} - \dfrac{1}{r + 4}$ (b) $\dfrac{n}{4(n + 4)}$ (c) $\dfrac{5}{168}$.

16. $\dfrac{2}{x} + \dfrac{1 - 2x}{x^2 + 1}$, $\dfrac{\pi}{12} + \ln\dfrac{3}{2}$.

17. (a) proof : show $\overrightarrow{PQ}.\overrightarrow{QR} = 0$

  (b) $\dfrac{x - 3}{1} = \dfrac{y + 1}{1} = \dfrac{z + 1}{6}$

  (c) no

  (d) $8x - 14y + z = 37$.

69

ESSENTIAL FORMULAE FOR ADVANCED HIGHER MATHS

Permutations and Combinations $^nP_r = \dfrac{n!}{(n-r)!}$ $^nC_r = \dfrac{n!}{r!(n-r)!}$

Pascal's Triangle

$$
\begin{array}{ccccccccccc}
 & & & & & 1 & & & & & \\
 & & & & 1 & & 1 & & & & \\
 & & & 1 & & 2 & & 1 & & & \\
 & & 1 & & 3 & & 3 & & 1 & & \\
 & 1 & & 4 & & 6 & & 4 & & 1 & \\
1 & & 5 & & 10 & & 10 & & 5 & & 1
\end{array}
$$

Binomial Theorem

$(a + x)^n = {}^nC_0 a^n x^0 + {}^nC_1 a^{n-1} x^1 + {}^nC_2 a^{n-2} x^2 + \ldots\ldots\ldots + {}^nC_{n-1} a^1 x^{n-1} + {}^nC_n a^0 x^n$

$= \displaystyle\sum_{r=0}^{n} {}^nC_r a^{n-r} x^r \quad T_{r+1} = {}^nC_r a^{n-r} x^r$

Partial Fractions

Let $\dfrac{ax + b}{(x + p)(x + q)} = \dfrac{A}{(x + p)} + \dfrac{B}{(x + q)} \quad \dfrac{ax + b}{(x + p)(x + q)(x + r)}$ etc.

Let $\dfrac{ax + b}{(x + p)^2} = \dfrac{A}{(x + p)} + \dfrac{B}{(x + p)^2}$

Let $\dfrac{ax^2 + bx + c}{(x + p)(x^2 + qx + r)} = \dfrac{A}{(x + p)} + \dfrac{Bx + C}{(x^2 + qx + r)}$ where $(x^2 + qx + r)$ is irreducible.

Note: if the degree of the numerator is at least that of the denominator, you have to divide out to obtain a proper fraction first before looking for partial fractions.

Trig Co-functions

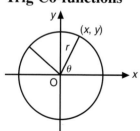

$\sin \theta = \dfrac{y}{r}$ $\operatorname{cosec} \theta = \dfrac{r}{y} = \dfrac{1}{\sin\theta}$ $\sin^2 \theta + \cos^2 \theta = 1$

$\cos \theta = \dfrac{x}{r}$ $\sec \theta = \dfrac{r}{x} = \dfrac{1}{\cos\theta}$ $\sec^2 \theta = 1 + \tan^2 \theta$

$\tan \theta = \dfrac{y}{x}$ $\cot \theta = \dfrac{x}{y} = \dfrac{1}{\tan\theta}$ $\operatorname{cosec}^2 \theta = 1 + \cot^2 \theta$

Standard Derivatives

Chain Rule

$$\frac{dy}{dx} = \frac{dy}{du} \times \frac{du}{dx}$$

Product Rule

$$D(uv) = uD(v) + vD(u)$$

Quotient Rule

$$D\left(\frac{u}{v}\right) = \frac{vD(u) - uD(v)}{v^2}$$

$D(\sin x) = \cos x$

$D(\cos x) = -\sin x$

$D(\tan x) = \sec^2 x$

$D(\operatorname{cosec} x) = -\operatorname{cosec} x \cot x$

$D(\sec x) = \sec x \tan x$

$D(\cot x) = -\operatorname{cosec}^2 x$

$$D(\sin^{-1} x) = \frac{1}{\sqrt{1 - x^2}}$$

$$D(\cos^{-1} x) = \frac{-1}{\sqrt{1 - x^2}}$$

$$D(\tan^{-1} x) = \frac{1}{1 + x^2}$$

$$D(e^x) = e^x \qquad D(\ln x) = \frac{1}{x}$$

Standard Integrals (without the "+c" in every case)

$$\int ax^n \, dx = \frac{ax^{n+1}}{n + 1} ; n \neq -1 \quad \int \frac{1}{x} \, dx = \ln x \quad \int e^x \, dx = e^x \quad \int \sec^2 x \, dx = \tan x$$

$$\int \sin x \, dx = -\cos x \qquad \int \cos x \, dx = \sin x \quad \int \tan x \, dx = \ln \sec x \quad \int \cot x \, dx = \ln \sin x$$

$$\int \frac{dx}{\sqrt{1 - x^2}} = \sin^{-1} x \qquad \int \frac{dx}{\sqrt{a^2 - x^2}} = \sin^{-1} \frac{x}{a} \qquad \int \frac{dx}{1 + x^2} = \tan^{-1} x$$

$$\int \frac{dx}{a^2 + x^2} = \frac{1}{a} \tan^{-1} \frac{x}{a} \qquad \int uD(v) \, dx = uv - \int vD(u) \, dx$$

De Moivre's Theorem $\qquad (\cos \theta + i \sin \theta)^n = \cos n\theta + i \sin n\theta$

Arithmetic Progressions $\quad T_n = a + (n - l)d \quad S_n = \frac{n}{2}(a + 1) = \frac{n}{2}[2a + (n - 1)d]$

Geometric Progressions

$$T_n = ar^{n-1} \qquad S_n = \frac{a(1 - r^n)}{1 - r} = \frac{a(r^n - 1)}{r - 1} \qquad S_\infty = \frac{a}{1 - r} ; |r| < 1$$

Matrices

$$A^{-1} = \frac{1}{ad - bc} \begin{pmatrix} d & -b \\ -c & a \end{pmatrix} \qquad \begin{vmatrix} a & b & c \\ d & e & f \\ g & h & i \end{vmatrix} = a \begin{vmatrix} e & f \\ h & i \end{vmatrix} - b \begin{vmatrix} d & f \\ g & i \end{vmatrix} + c \begin{vmatrix} d & e \\ g & h \end{vmatrix}$$

Vectors $\mathbf{a} \times \mathbf{b} = |\mathbf{a}||\mathbf{b}| \sin \theta \mathbf{n}$ where θ is the angle between the positive directions of $\mathbf{a}$ and $\mathbf{b}$, and $\mathbf{n}$ is a unit vector such that $\mathbf{a}, \mathbf{b}, \mathbf{n}$ form a right-handed system.

$$[\mathbf{a}, \mathbf{b}, \mathbf{c}] = \text{the scalar triple product} = \mathbf{a}.(\mathbf{b} \times \mathbf{c}) = \begin{vmatrix} a_1 & a_2 & a_2 \\ b_1 & b_2 & b_3 \\ c_1 & c_2 & c_3 \end{vmatrix}$$

equation of a plane $ax + by + cz = d$ [direction vector $a\mathbf{i} + b\mathbf{j} + c\mathbf{k}$]

equations of a line $\dfrac{x - x_1}{a} = \dfrac{y - y_1}{b} = \dfrac{z - z_1}{c} = t$

[through (x_1, y_1, z_1) parallel to $a\mathbf{i} + b\mathbf{j} + c\mathbf{k}$]

vector equation of a line $\mathbf{r} = \mathbf{a} + t\mathbf{u}$ or $\mathbf{r} = (1 - t)\mathbf{a} + t\mathbf{b}$

vector equation of a plane $\mathbf{r} = \mathbf{a} + t\mathbf{b} + u\mathbf{c}$
or $\mathbf{r} = (1 - t - u)\mathbf{a} + t\mathbf{b} + u\mathbf{c}$

Maclaurin's expansion $f(x) = f(0) + xf'(0) + x^2 \dfrac{f''(0)}{2} + x^3 \dfrac{f'''(0)}{3} + \dots.$

Differential Equations

first order linear $\dfrac{dy}{dx} + P(x)y = Q(x)$ I.F. $= e^{\int P(x)dx}$

second order homogeneous $ay'' + by' + cy = 0$
try $y = Ae^{mx}$ distinct roots   equal roots   complex roots
    $y = Ae^{m_1x} + Be^{m_2x}$ $y = (Ax + B)e^{mx}$ $y = e^{mx}(A \cos nx + B \sin nx)$

second order non-homogeneous $ay'' + by' + cy = f(x)$

$y = $ complementary function $+$ particular integral
(homog. Solution $+$ find by inspection)

Proof by Induction: these should be known

$$\sum_{r=1}^{n} 1 = n \qquad \sum_{r=1}^{n} r = \frac{1}{2}n(n + 1) \qquad \sum_{r=1}^{n} r^2 = \frac{1}{6}n(n + 1)(2n + 1)$$

Proof by Induction: of interest

$$\sum_{r=1}^{n} r^3 = \frac{1}{4}n^2(n + 1)^2$$

72